THE EDUCATION
OF A
POKER PIGEON

ALSO BY ANONYMOUS

Play Poker Like a Pigeon (and Take the Money Home)

Published by Lyle Stuart Books

THE EDUCATION OF A POKER PIGEON

SECRETS LEARNED FROM A LIFE IN HIGH-STAKES POKER

Anonymous

LYLE STUART

Kensington Publishing Corp.
www.kensingtonbooks.com

LYLE STUART BOOKS are published by

Kensington Publishing Corp.
850 Third Avenue
New York, NY 10022

All Kensington titles, imprints, and distributed lines are available at special quantity discounts for bulk purchases for sales promotions, premiums, fund-raising, educational, or institutional use. Special book excerpts or customized printings can also be created to fit specific needs. For details, write or phone the office of the Kensington special sales manager: Kensington Publishing Corp., 850 Third Avenue, New York, NY 10022, attn: Special Sales Department; phone 1-800-221-2647.

Lyle Stuart is a trademark of Kensington Publishing Corp.

First printing: March 2008

10 9 8 7 6 5 4 3 2 1

Printed in the United States of America

ISBN-13: 978-0-8184-0719-2
ISBN-10: 0-8184-0719-0

Contents

Author's Note

Other than the autobiographical data, every single event described herein I either personally witnessed or learned about from someone I have absolute confidence in as a source with the exception of those events that I have identified as suspect (an example of a suspect item would be the Titanic Thompson tales of which I am unsure, and stories told by Jimmy Chagra that I seriously doubt because of my long-ago acquaintance with the man). As for the autobiographical data, overall, my life story is true as told, though forty-plus years of recollections might be dim enough for me to get certain events out of order. Where I've changed certain people's names, identified other people by pseudonyms, or slightly altered some events, I haven't done so through any desire to protect the innocent; some of the folks told about are still alive and kicking and might not want their true identities revealed, and I have intentionally altered some events because, were the stories dead-on right down the line, certain old poker pros would know in a heartbeat who actually wrote this book, and protection of my anonymity as an author is a dead serious business with me. The poker tips are given in the heartfelt desire that they will assist you; you'll run across so-called experts who will disagree with my strategies just as I disagree with theirs, but that's all part of the ball game, and which advice you wish to follow is certainly up to you. Descriptions I've given of the poker life in general are pretty much the way things are.

THE EDUCATION OF A
POKER PIGEON

1

I Don't Want to Write What You Want to Read

I want to fulfill a lifelong dream and write my autobiography.

You want to read a book chock-full of tips that will help make you a better poker player.

So, are we just banging our heads together? Or tugging away in opposite directions, accomplishing zero?

No way. We'll meet both goals. It's doable. Trust me.

Come on, you don't have to be polite. If the exciting tale of how I morphed from an economics major with a brilliant future into a king-of-the-road, leave-town-ahead-of-the-sheriff poker bum won't keep you on the edge of your seat, say so. After all, it's your nickel that we're spending here.

So how 'bout if we compromise? Suppose I sort of write my life story while I slip little poker instruction tidbits into each chapter, or strategy lessons explaining my play in this hand or that hand against this or that big-time professional, and also sprinkle the book with history lessons on the development of Texas Hold 'Em and why it's caught on as the only poker game worth knowing right now and (best of all) put forth some ideas on improving your poker lifestyle that, in the long run, will serve you better than any instruction on when to call, raise, bluff, or fold can ever hope to. I can even include tips on how to detect cheating, and how to spot a game that has a better than even chance of getting robbed by masked folks toting shotguns, so that thereafter you can avoid such games and thus reduce your risk of having your pocket picked or getting shot by hijackers. How 'bout if I do all that? Huh?

What's that? Now you might be interested? I thought so.

Look, I don't care if you're teaching high-level chess strategy or basic toilet repair; the best tool for the teacher to use is his or her experience. I'm still going to advocate disguising yourself as a big fat sucker at the poker table, the same advice that I gave when writing *Play Poker Like a Pigeon (and Take the Money Home)*, but, just as I said in that book, putting the pigeon image across takes a great deal of know-how about professional play. By outlining the steps that took me from a pure novice to a pro-level player, I can help you to avoid the pitfalls that I've experienced and thus put your learning process in warp-speed mode. If you know the right roads in advance, you can eliminate a lot of wrong turns and accelerate your game to a higher level in a much shorter span than it took me.

That's the answer, isn't it? Now I have your full attention. I'm going to entertain you with a few life-experience-type stories while I give you more insights into the intricacies of the game than you ever thought possible.

Okay, you say, *maybe you've got something there. But gimme a for instance.*

Well here's a for instance. There was the time, way back when, that I looked up from the poker table to see a guy dressed up like a monkey pointing a sawed-off, over-and-under, double-barreled shotgun in my direction, and that's when I made the lightning quick decision to lie facedown on the floor. Or the time when—

Jesus Christ, you pipe up, that's what all the buildup was about? Who wouldn't know to hit the deck with a shotgun staring them in the face? That's no big revelation, and it has zilch to do with how to play poker.

Okay, I'll grant that you might have a point, but I don't think that anyone else could have gone facedown with the *panache* that I did, or that anyone else could've made the decision to do so nearly as quickly. And that's what poker's all about—making lightning quick decisions under fire.

The hijacking example might be a bit hokey, but I've always advocated the lifestyle side of the poker player as more important than any playing skill, and I'll continue to do so until they tote me away from the card room table feetfirst. Plain vanilla how-to-play-poker lessons will no more make a winner out of you than Tiger Woods's swing tips will put you in Sunday contention at the Masters. There's a guy on every golf course in America cruising around daily in sixty-five strokes who hits it just as far as Tiger and usually putts like a haint as well (that's "haint" as in "haunt," a little Southern colloquialism for you-all Yankees, meaning that the guy putts like a ghost, likely the ghost of Bobby Locke or someone similar), but instead of playing the back nine at Augusta on a Sunday in April, this guy hustles people for ten bucks a side and, on the few occasions when he loses, sneaks off into the parking lot to make his getaway while his opponents hang around the clubhouse waiting to get paid. At each and every poker tournament you'll run into the same sort of thing, a string of people who claim to be pros standing around looking for a playing stake or meal handout, and most of those people will know just as much about how to play poker as Hellmuth, Brunson, Harrington, or anyone else in the room. Knowing what cards to play and how to play 'em amounts to about 10 percent of the total picture; controlling one's emotions and managing one's money take up the other 90 percent, and consistent winners understand very well that overall smart living is a thousand times more important than knowing the odds of J10 beating AK in a hand of Texas Hold 'Em. So while I do intend to give you a few playing tips, the more astute among you will pay more attention to the lifestyle suggestions than the playing strategies I'll go into.

So to summarize: **In trying to make a living playing poker— or if not trying to support yourself, at least being in it strictly for profit and not for the Wednesday night circle jerk with "the guys"—how you manage your life and money is head and shoulders more important that how much you're lucky enough to win.** That's basic my-old-Daddy-told-me-so strategy, right up there with instruction on how to put on your shoes and brush your teeth, and this advice works in playing poker for profit just as it works in any other path that you might choose between the womb and the grave.

See what I mean?

You don't?

Christ, getting this project off the ground is going to take a little salesmanship. Well, anything that's worth doing is also worth some effort, so maybe I'd better quit acting like the Geico gecko with the jokes and whatnot and get serious.

So consider this (try to picture me assuming a somber expression and going into full-blown teacher mode here): Just about everything that we use today to advance our business acumen or playtime pleasure is the product of evolution that came about as a means to solving a problem, and the game of poker is no exception. The cell phone exists because, in all probability, once upon a time Alexander Graham Bell wanted to talk to his maid without running all over the house trying to find her. In Jolly

Old Germany, Johann Gutenberg likely got sick of reproducing manuscripts by hand, so he invented the moveable type that over time evolved into the typewriter and, eventually, Microsoft Word. And in poker's dim dark ages, game runners saw more customers waiting for seats than were actually playing, so they built oblong tables set for ten and—*poof*—invented Texas Hold 'Em.

Really. Add it up. In five-card draw or five-card stud, thirty-five cards come off the deck in a seven-handed game during the deal (and who hasn't played in some Wednesday night games with "the guys" where no one ever folds and where in order for everyone to draw the dealer ends up shuffling the discards?). In Hold 'Em each player starts out with only two cards, the board consists of only five, and even when Hold 'Em is played ten-handed only half the deck comes into play during a hand. (Here I should point out that opposed to today, where the house cuts each pot for a certain amount—in most legal casino games, state laws prohibit a rake of more than four dollars a hand—old-time backroom game runners "took time." "Taking time" meant that each player had to pay so much periodically in order to keep his seat. Normally this figure was five dollars an hour, with the runner collecting two dollars on the half hour and three dollars on the hour from each player at the table, so by increasing the number of players from seven to ten, the game runners raised their take from thirty-five to fifty dollars an hour, a *43 percent increase*.) While Hold 'Em does owe its existence to old-time game runners' greed, modern house games have benefited as well, because a hand of Hold 'Em takes up, on average, less than half the time consumed in a hand of any other form of poker. If you're cutting the pot for four dollars a hand, and you can double the number of hands played per hour, you can double your take as well. So greed rules poker just as it rules banking, but as we all learn as we go through life, greed ain't all bad.

Not surprisingly, when Texas Hold 'Em first came to pass,

there was no such thing as a good Hold 'Em player, because the probabilities and strategies in Hold 'Em were so different from those in any other form of poker. Other than a certain amount of inherent card sense, there is no similarity whatsoever between a good poker player and a good *Hold 'Em* player, and the exceptional Hold 'Em players evolved over time by taking note of the differences between Hold 'Em and other games and learning how to turn those differences to their advantage. Many years ago I knew the legendary Titanic Thompson for a time— come on, I'm not *that* fucking old; he was in his seventies and I was in my twenties the first time I ever laid eyes on the guy— and in addition to his reputation for being one of the greatest on-the-spot odds figurers who ever lived, Ti was a brilliant Hold 'Em player, and trust me that the two skills are closely related.

I did a chapter in *Play Poker Like a Pigeon* called "The Odd-ball Odds of Texas Hold 'Em," where I elaborated on the differences between figuring odds in Hold 'Em versus figuring odds in other forms of poker and explained in detail why these differences exist. Well, some of the information in this book will be a repeat of what I discussed in the other book, but here I hope to broaden your perspective. I'm going to tell the story of how, early on, I jumped into Hold 'Em games that were far over my head, and, by learning how to compute the odds of this or that happening, eventually adjusted my thinking from stud and draw until I became a pretty fair hand at Hold 'Em as well. And that, dear reader, is the main way that I'm going to shorten your road; if you're already hip to the differences between Hold 'Em and other poker games, you're more than halfway there before you ever take a seat in a casino card room. And if you're one of the myriad players who are consistent winners at stud and draw but can't seem to break through as a Hold 'Em guy, then the lessons in this book are going to be right up your alley.

Now then, am I beginning to hook you? Of course I am.

So here's a final teaser before we move on to the meat of the subject. Another riveting example of what this book holds in store for you has to do with the development of Hold 'Em terminology (and who doesn't want to learn the lingo required to be a really hip and with-it Big-Time Poker Guy, even though as a practicing resident of Pigeonville you shouldn't advertise that you know any of this stuff). If you've started to play quite a bit of Hold 'Em, you've doubtless noticed that older players use different terminology than you hear on ESPN during the World Series. To the real veterans, the "turn" is what the youngsters call the "flop," and what you now know as the "turn" and "river" cards used to be called Fourth Street and Fifth Street. Well the old-time terminology is actually proper Hold 'Emspeak, and the latter-day terms only exist due to the hustlers' desire to draw the suckers into the game. Old-time Hold 'Em hustlers, while they spoke Hold 'Emese quite fluently among themselves, used stud examples in sucking in the pigeons so that it wouldn't occur to the sucker how different the two games really are. Seven-card stud back then was called "Down the River," a name first heard on southbound pleasure boats along the Mississippi. The "turn" card in Down the River was the first upcard (after the two face-down hole cards), and the "river" card was the final card in the hand, always dealt facedown. So the old thieves indoctrinated the pigeons by telling them that in Hold 'Em the first card dealt after the flop was just like the "turn" card in Down the River, and were thus encouraged to use the same strategy that had worked for them in Down the River, even though using seven-card stud strategy in Hold 'Em is certain suicide. *Come on in, Mr. Pigeon, the water's fine,* the old-timers may as well have said.

Have I gotcha yet? If I haven't, I'll bet I'm getting close. So you just try to keep from turning the page to the next chapter.

Just try; I dare you. But before you turn the page, do one more little thing. Carry this book up to the cash register, fork over, and add the book to your poker library. This ain't Snake Oil we're selling; it's the real fucking thing. It's cheap at twice the price, and in the long run, you'll be glad that you did.

2

Don't Shoot—I Fold Already

The monkey who was holding the shotgun told me to lie facedown. I was a blur of motion as I got down on the floor and buried my nose in the carpet. Actually the monkey wasn't really a monkey; he was a squatty guy in jeans and a plain white T-shirt, and he only looked like a monkey because he was wearing an ape mask. Or at least that's what I later heard from other hijack victims. I saw only a furry face, a blunt snout with huge nostrils, and sawed-off double barrels the size of teacups. For all I know the guy might really have been *a monkey.*

I'd no sooner done as told than the monkey's buddy straddled me, reached into my pockets and took my roll of hundred-dollar bills, then tied my wrists behind me using plastic zip cuffs. The monkey's buddy wore a monkey mask as well. Later, when discussing the incident with the cops, I'd refer to this pair as Monkey One and Monkey Two. Monkey One wore a chimpanzee mask while Monkey Two had dressed up as a gorilla. The two uniformed policemen who took the report didn't think that I was funny. Today I probably wouldn't think that I was funny, either, but back then I had a million of 'em.

I fell victim to the monkeys as I sat alone at the poker table, having come in early to set up in preparation for our nightly illegal game. My partner in crime and I were running the game, chopping the pot for six or seven hundred bucks a night and splitting the profits. We provided rent, utilities, cards, chips, pro-style padded poker table, and food and drinks for the players, and I believe that our total monthly nut came to less than one night's take from cutting the pot. We were also supposed to provide security. In this instance we seemed to have fumbled the ball. As I lay there trembling, I promised God that if he'd let me live through this day I'd never draw another breath outside the law. I suspect that God doubted my sincerity. Given my history, I wouldn't have blamed Him if He had.

The first time I ever gambled was once in high school, when three basketball players separated me from twenty-five dollars on the team bus playing a Cajun game called Boo Ray. To get some idea of what twenty-five dollars amounted to in those days, please know this: I earned my spending money during the summer changing tires in hundred-degree heat for seventy-five cents an hour. I worked sixty-hour weeks from June through August, and my weekly take-home pay was just a shade over thirty-eight bucks. Also on point: Back then we could go to the movies for sixty cents, and the first new car that my father ever bought—a 1955 Buick Super with a Dynaflo transmission—cost thirty-four hundred dollars. Daddy—a pillar of the Church of Christ who didn't approve of gambling, and who wouldn't have bet that fat meat was greasy if his life depended on the outcome—got a sizeable bonus on his job during my senior year, which pushed his income all the way up to a grand a month. Twenty-five bucks to a high school kid in the 1950s was a *ton* of money.

The game we were playing, Boo Ray, is a bastard child of five-card draw and bridge, where each player antes a given sum (for us it was a quarter, though in later life I've seen Boo Ray games with hundred-dollar antes and many thousands at stake) before every hand. Then the dealer gives everyone five cards and, during the deal, turns one of his own cards faceup without first looking at it. The dealer's exposed card becomes the trump suit for that hand. Then everyone declares in or out, and everyone who's in gets to draw up to a complete five-card hand. The player to the dealer's left then leads, and everyone else must follow suit—unless, of course, the player is out of the required suit, in which case the player can trump just as in the game of bridge. Only in Boo Ray there is no sloughing off; if you don't have the led suit, you must trump, and if someone else has already trumped before you and you're also out of the led suit, you must overtrump if you can. The player taking the most tricks wins the pot. If anyone plays in the hand and fails to take a single trick, that person is said to have Boo Rayed and is required to match the pot prior to the next hand being played. In case you haven't already figured it out, Boo Ray is the most cutthroat card game known to man.

Losing that twenty-five dollars to my basketball-playing buddies was the best thing that ever happened to me, for several reasons. First of all, the incident caused me to think—boy, did it ever!—and, let's face it, deep thinking isn't a normal high school pastime. For a few nights I lay awake counting the cracks in the ceiling, worrying about dipping into my college tuition savings in order to ante up what I'd lost. About four days later the three guys whom I owed cornered me in the gym and gave me a little talking-to, and for a couple of nights after that I lay awake worrying about what my student-athlete creditors would do to me if I didn't come across. Finally, I bit the bullet, went to the bank with my tail between my legs, withdrew the money, carried the cash to school, and caused great joy on the basketball team by making the eagle fly.

As I watched my money disappear into the guys' tight-assed blue jeans as they walked away with cheerleaders on their arms, I was already forming, in the back of my mind, what would later become **The Poker Pigeon's Ultimate Gambling Postulate Number One: If you're gonna play, you gotta pay.**

This postulate may seem so basic that expressing it in words may seem a waste of time, but remembering the Boo Ray incident has stood me in good stead many times throughout my life, and for the past forty years or so I've made it a practice to never play any card game on credit. If you pay off on the spot and owe no one in the game, forgetting about your losses and going on with your life will be easier, and you will never be in the nail-biting position of owing money that you're unable to pay. I've been offered credit in both casino card rooms and private games and, based on that first experience back in high school with those minor-league versions of Shaq, Kobe, and Magic, I've always declined and am glad that I have.

And what does all this have to do with playing good poker? Plenty.

Playing top-flight poker requires a clear mind and, above all, plenty of patience, and those two attributes are by far more important than any knowledge of odds or foxy strategies. If you're playing in a game with any sort of high-level stakes (and the definition of high-level stakes changes from player to player depending on the size of the player's bankroll), and you're in debt from some previous game and need really fast cash in order to settle up, desperation is going to ruin the quality of your play. I've never seen an exception to this rule. I've seen players who *claimed* that they were exceptions, and who swore that money meant nothing to them and that they could play well under any set of circumstances, but every one of those guys, when push came to shove, turned out not to be telling the truth. If you're playing on money that you owe elsewhere, then you're going to be desperate, period. A desperate poker player, unfortunately, is also a *really lousy* poker player. Period, paragraph, very truly yours.

Postulate Number One goes not only for people just now

learning the game; it goes double for so-called professional poker players. A large number of pros spend more time ducking creditors than practicing their chosen calling, and I think that's because they confuse settling their poker obligations with the chicken-and-egg question: Which comes first? If the poker pro is in debt, the only way that he has to pay is to continue to play, or at least that's what he keeps telling himself. If he settles up what he owes he will then be out of money and unable to get in a game, so the situation where poker creditors wait futilely on their money while the one who owes is in a game across town—or, in modern jet-set times, across the country or even across the world—playing for cash grows more common every year. I can't tell you how many really expert poker players I've known who've disappeared from the scene because they were so far in debt that they couldn't show their faces, but I can tell you—and count on my fingers and toes—the full name of every single poker player I know who has been around for more than ten years and is still playing, and without exception those people don't make a practice of owing money. Some have that old ace in the hole (that's a person outside the poker world whom they can count on to furnish them a bankroll when a case of the shorts rears its head) while a few others have the discipline, when they're out of money, to quit playing altogether and work at a job—dealing poker, driving a cab, or whatever—until they can put together another grubstake. Opposed to what many self-conceived sharpies think, there is no shame in taking on a job until you've replenished your poker funds.

And here's a little aside to those of you who have begun to yawn while thinking, *Christ, anyone ought to know not to gamble on credit*: What's grammar school–level stuff in the regular world becomes think-tank material in the poker world. If you stick to the Wednesday night games with "the guys," then you're probably never going to have any credit problems, but if you're only interested in "the guys" and their midweek games, then what the hell are you reading my stuff for? This book is not for beginners or casual players; it's for serious poker people who play with a strict profit motive, and who are interested in moving up to the next level. Whether you play in casinos or in backroom games where house-run poker isn't legal, you're going to run into seemingly "nice" guys who need a loan until tomorrow, and if your experience is in "the guys' " Wednesday night get-togethers where the players are mostly legitimate folks, you're going to be tempted to loan it to them. Well, if you do, write off the money because you've seen the last of it, and you've also seen the last of the guy, because he's going to be ducking you from now on. If you're like me and grew up in a principled environment, in playing pro-level poker you'll run into people with a different set of values than you've ever experienced. A large number of card room regulars are gambling addicts who will lie, cheat, steal, or murder—that's right, I said murder—in order to get the money to keep on playing, and if you play in that world, you must keep your eyes and ears open at all times.

Choose your illegal back-street card rooms very carefully, because those are unregulated places that might simply stiff you just as an individual almost surely will. My first foray into no-limit poker came about in the 1960s, when I was playing in an illegal house ten- and twenty-dollar limit game that went on in the same room as a "big" game featuring some of the most famous poker players in the world. I'd done really well in the ten-and-twenty game, and one day as I was cashing in my chips I glanced over at the Scoot table (for all of you rookies, "Scoot" was what we called no-limit poker in those days, meaning that at any time you could "scoot" your entire bankroll into the pot) and found a seat open. I'd just won enough for a no-limit buy-in and so, thinking "what the hell" to myself, I carried my winnings over to the big-timers' game and flopped into the empty seat. The poker all-Americans looked at me, then at each other. I think one guy even snickered.

About an hour later I'd become the poker hustlers' nightmare, the pigeon on a roll who wins big in spite of some of the worst play imaginable. I'll never forget this one particular hand where I took a 35 of spades into a raised pot, caught two 3s on the flop, and then busted two players by checking and then going all in when one of the other guys fired a bet my way. I remember that one guy ripped his two aces in half after that hand, and the house had to come up with a new deck before the game could go on.

The hourlong session resulted in a twenty-five-hundred dollar win (though I'm sure that if I'd sat there long enough I would have gone home broke), more money than I'd ever seen in one place at the time, and, punch-drink with success, I showed the good judgment to quit. I staggered over to the cashier's podium with so many chips that I dropped half of them on the floor and had to go back to pick them up. I set my chips on the counter, placed them in neat five-hundred-dollar stacks, stood back, and waited for my money.

The game runner/cashier was a small-time penitentiary refugee with multiple tats on both arms (this was the '60s, when tattoos appeared only on convicts and sailors who'd gotten drunk on shore leave, and shapely tattooed butts were unheard of). He leaned over the counter and said in a whisper, "Look, I'll have to cash you in tomorrow. I gotta bring it from home, okay?"

The arrangement sounded strange to me at first, but after all this was *the place*, the spot where the big boys played. After I thought about it, it made perfect sense to me that large sums were kept in an impenetrable safe at a secret location, so I went my merry way and *didn't even collect the money I'd used to buy into the limit game in the beginning!*

Wide-eyed and stupid, huh? Sure, but it didn't take all that long for me to know better.

Three months later I was still unpaid, even though—and you gotta forgive my hardheadedness here since I was young and a virgin and all that—I'd actually come back to play in the same joint every day in the interim, and while I'd stuck to the limit game that held to its cash-in, chips-out format, my constant grousing over being owed was like water off a duck's back to Tattooed Man. No matter how hard I'd beg, he'd just come up with another story—anywhere from "Damn, I forgot" to an imagined burglary at his place where thieves made off with his loot—to put me off for still another day. And to give credit where credit was due, the fault didn't lie entirely with the tattooed guy; I later learned that the reason he was so short of money was that he'd extended credit to some of the all-stars playing in the no-limit game, and believe me, as I learned in later years, trying to collect from some of those guys was a waste of time.

I'd given up hope of ever seeing my money when one day I nearly fainted from shock when, as I cashed in my chips from the limit game, Tattooed Man handed me a hundred-dollar bill over and above my chip count. He told me that he was determined to pay off my no-limit winnings no matter how long it took, and that while he still hadn't collected what he was owed by the poker all-stars, business had picked up and he could come across with a little every day. What he offered was better than nothing, of course, so I pocketed the hundred, smiled, and went on my way.

My hope of getting my money on a payout didn't last long either, however, because the very next day Tattooed Man's game fell victim to a police bust (I heard that another player who'd failed to get his money tipped off the cops, but I've got no proof of that), Tattooed Man himself had his parole revoked for running an illegal house game, and the poker joint closed for good. I've never seen Tattooed Man since, and, honestly, long ago I wrote off the money as a learning expense.

What's my point other than that I was awfully dumb in those

days? Just this: legal casino card rooms are secure places where you can play and have no worry about collecting your winnings, but before you play in any backroom illegal game, check out the game runners. This isn't hard to do, because you'll know someone who knows someone, as is always the case in the poker world, and there is nothing that gamblers enjoy more than giving crappy credit reports where crappy credit reports are due. In the foregoing instance, I assumed that everything was on the up-and-up, because I'd heard of the Big-Time Poker Guys who played in the joint, and there is no truer saying than the one that goes like this: When you *assume*, you make an *ass* out of *u* and *me*.

Winning at poker is hard enough without adding the possibility of getting stiffed to the list of hazards, and not only that, people who are strapped for cash are the ones most likely to cheat you. Play for cash and cash only, and then only in places where you are 100 percent sure that the folks running the game won't screw you. If you have a whisper of doubt, other games are right down the block and just too easy to find.

When I first launched into this discourse, I was about to outline the things I learned from losing twenty-five bucks to some basketball players back in high school, and while I may have gone around the block a couple of times, I think I've gotten the development of the aforementioned Poker Pigeon's Ultimate Gambling Postulate Number One out of the way. Okay, done with Number One. Let's go on to the other things I learned while brooding over my hard-earned-but-mine-no-longer summer tire-changing money, yea these many years ago.

The Poker Pigeon's Ultimate Gambling Postulate Number Two: **In choosing places to play, in protecting your money, or in any other facet of the poker business, never let celebrity get in your eye.**

And now you're probably thinking, *Is this guy crazy? To begin with I don't know any celebrities, and if I did, they sure as hell*

*wouldn't be sitting in on a poker game where I'm playing. I'm
chucking this book into the garbage can, right now, and finding
something to read that's gonna tell me when to raise and when to
fold instead of pumping me full of bullshit that happened back in
the 1950s when this moron was in high school. Christ, maybe the
guy has Alzheimer's or something.*

Well, I'll confess that my memory isn't what it was, and I
won't comment on whether I'm crazy or not, but I told you in
the beginning that I was going to give you some poker-playing
lifestyle tips, and this one is *big*. This is one of the life lessons
that are more important than any tips on playing strategy, okay?
Just keep your seat and listen up.

I went to a high school run by jockstraps, just like the high
school that you probably attended, and although these three basketball heroes were guys you never heard of, please believe that hearts
raced and panties dropped to the floor whenever they swam through
their own little minnow-filled pond. As the lowly team manager
I was totally in awe of these superstars of the student body, and
when they paid me enough attention to invite me to play cards
on the team bus with them, I jumped at the chance. To top it
off they lured me in by saying that the stakes were "only" a
quarter a hand, when all three of them had played Boo Ray and
knew that the total that I could lose was many times that amount.

And, oh, yeah, they cheated.

I discovered the cheating part too late, after I'd already de-
pleted my bank account in order to pay off, when another basketball team member took pity on me and told me that these guys
had passed each other cards when I wasn't looking, and that the
game was a setup from the get-go—the result of letting people
know too much about my work habits; none of these guys ever
lifted a finger during the summer to earn a buck, and since they
all knew about my own job and bank account, they had it figured, rightfully, that I was the one-in-a-million sucker who would

actually pay them after they cheated me. And not only that, they were using their tale of plucking me for twenty-five dollars as a great source of amusement around the locker room, so not only was I out the money, but I was also awash in public shame. I was stunned that these godlike heroes would resort to cheating, but I did take note for future reference. Did I ever.

And now you're thinking, *So some guys screwed you back in high school. So what?*

So this. If you're contemplating taking a stroll through the casino-based poker world, you're going to come in contact at some point with celebrity. Take my word that there isn't any way around it. Movie stars and sports heroes have caught the poker bug along with the rest of the country, and ESPN has made public figures out of many former down-and-out poker vagabonds, and one day you'll look across the table and recognize someone from his or her image on the TV or movie screen—or if you don't recognize the person on sight, at least his or her name will be one you've heard. In the past year alone I have sat in on games or have stood in the same card rooms with Tobey Maguire, James Woods, Larry Flynt, Alex Rodriguez, Doyle Brunson, and other people whose names are pretty much household words, and although most of these folks are really decent people, some are just the opposite. This is especially true of the poker bums turned celebrities, whose fortune seldom equals their fame, though there are also some insufferable sports and entertainment figures who believe that the public owes them something merely for being allowed to hover about in the same room with them.

As for the high school basketball stars, well, later on in the same school year the situation was reversed, in a poker game where I'd gotten a thousand times smarter than I was when we played Boo Ray on the bus. I was the big winner in the poker game, while all three of these guys lost their asses on credit, just as they should have, because they were such bad poker players, and I ended up with three substantial markers for my trouble. And did these guys run to the bank for the money to pay *me*? Why, hell no, they didn't, though they did wave at me with one hand while hugging a cheerleader with the other as they passed me in the hall for the rest of that spring. That was more than forty years ago and I've yet to see my winnings, but I did have the satisfaction of writing the following note in each of their annuals at the end of the school year: "Thanks for the card-playing lesson and for the memories." I meant it, too. Knowing those three guys gave me the best experience I could have gotten at that age, and I'll benefit from what they taught me forever.

The high school chain of events saved me several hundred dollars before I'd been playing high-stakes poker more than a couple of years. I was living in Dallas and playing in a game in the Oak Cliff section of town when one of our regulars, a minor league baseball player, showed up one night with a well-known television actor in tow. This prime-time star was on a show that was every bit as big as *ER* and *Law & Order* are today, and to get some idea of the way the players felt, try to equate this incident with George Clooney showing up unannounced and taking a seat in the game where you regularly play. This guy and his entourage of producers and writers had come to Texas to film an episode in the Dallas area. The local newspapers were full of the cast and crew's daily activities, and there, all of a sudden—*boom*—stood the star in real life, hunting for a little poker action. Hard-line gamblers morphed at once into wide-eyed and tongue-tied celebrity fans, and I confess that I was as overcome with awe as any of the rest of the poker crowd present that night.

But I wasn't quite as gullible, largely due to my experience with the high school basketball stars.

Not only was the famous actor handsome and self-assured, but he never saw a poker hand that he wasn't in love with or a bet that he wouldn't call. Christ, I don't believe he folded once for several hours, and I remember that when he finally *did* toss one of his hands into the discards, my palms itched with desire and it was all I could do to keep from snatching up those cards to see what the fuck there could possibly be that this guy *wouldn't* play. Though he came in with a pocketful of cash, our TV star was broke before the game was two hours old.

And that's when the real playacting began, and, hey, truth be told, the players in the game left themselves wide open for what was to follow. The TV star never really asked for credit, and I believe he didn't because he'd been in this situation so often that he knew he wouldn't have to. When he ran out of cash he fumbled in his pockets, looked surprised, and merely said, "I guess that's going to have to be it for me, boys. I seem to be out of money."

I laugh every time I think of the scene, where all of these so-called prudent poker players tried to run over each other in a race to see who'd be first to give their money away to this guy. First, one of the players said, "Hey, your credit's damned sure good with me," while forking over a couple hundred. Then when the actor lost *that* money, there was someone else in line ready to take the first guy's place, and so on and so forth until the actor was in the players' pockets for a thousand dollars or more.

Oh, and as for me? Well, when I sensed the way things were going that night, I cashed in my chips and excused myself from the game. For the next year or so I listened in secret pleasure to the bitching from the actor's poker creditors, and to the stories of the strategies they used in trying to collect from the guy (and you won't appreciate this tale until you've tried to fight your way through agents and publicists in an attempt to so much as speak in person to one of these paparazzi magnets). The poker players weren't the only losers in town by a long shot; several department stores had extended credit to the show's cast and crew during the time of the shoot, and to my knowledge these stores were never paid a dime. I did hear one of the department store moguls say—during a poker game, of course, since department store moguls like to gamble as much as the next person—that the advertisement his business received for having the television folks shopping in the store was worth far more than the money he lost, but I believe with all my heart that he was rationalizing. No one who's gotten stiffed could possibly have been as jolly as the department store guy pretended to be.

By the way, the TV show continued on the air for about three more seasons, and one of the poker game regulars who played Santa for the actor that night swears that one time when he was in his cups, he threw a full can of beer and smashed his television screen right in the middle of one of the star's poignant monologues. I didn't witness the incident, but I do believe the guy.

Now let's talk about celebrity in a different light, specifically with regard to cheating. So, okay, I might be a bit overboard with this segment in speculating who you might or might not run into in your forays through the poker world. You might play poker every day for the rest of your life and never stumble into a game with the *Ocean's Eleven* cast, and you might not ever look up to find one of the poker stars you've seen on ESPN or Fox Sports Net sitting across the table. But in just about every serious game you play in for the first time, there's going to be a local poker hero who is every bit as much a celebrity among his own peers as a movie star is to the rest of the world. One thing about celebrities, they know they're famous and take advantage of that fact. The local poker star is going to have some of his buddies along, and from the moment they lay eyes on you they'll try to intimidate you out of your money. They'll gang up to run bluffs against you, putting you in the middle and raising back and forth when one of the raisers is holding next to nothing, and their Number One goal will be to put you in your place and make you afraid of them. If they can successfully instill fear and/or intimidation, there is no way that you are going to walk away from the table a winner, because you'll underplay your good hands and toss a lot of winners away when faced with multiple raises.

These ganging-up tactics come with and without barefaced cheating. I'll stick to my guns in restating that casino card rooms are the safest place to play and that you'll never be stiffed or cheated in a casino *by casino personnel*, but the Honest Abe bit doesn't go for the individual players you'll run into in legal card rooms. More often than not, the guys who are in cahoots won't stick cards up their sleeves or have a guy holding a mirrored tray behind you so that they can see your pocket cards; they will simply pay attention to what's happening in the game and watch for prearranged signals. When one of their group bets, it's the partner in crime's duty to raise at least once and then take his next cue from the original bettor's reaction. If the original bettor raises the bet even higher, then that's the signal for the crossfire blitzkrieg to begin with you playing the part of London and the poker sharpies the Nazis. I've heard rationalizations from self-imagined poker sharks to the effect that "it ain't cheating unless you start holding out cards, passing them to each other or something," but I wholeheartedly disagree. Poker is a game of individual skill, not a team event, and any scenario where two or more players are splitting their winnings and losses, ganging up on their competitors, and acting on their hands in conjunction with what their partners are doing is crooked as hell and should be subject to fines and jail terms.

The awful truth, however, is that while casinos watch over cheating in house games such as craps and blackjack like Jesus over his flock, card room personnel are going to do little with regard to stopping cheating unless (1) the cheating is so blatant that customers can both recognize the cheating and prove that it exists, or (2) said cheating is going to cost the casino money. In poker no one plays against the house and the house profits the same no matter who wins. And when players are ganging up on you, as previously discussed, there is simply no proof that the boys are doing anything wrong, and you have only your experience and instincts on which to base your suspicion. In rare, rare instances there will be actual card manipulation, but no card tricks can work unless the house dealer is in on the scam. And this does happen, though not often, because in states where gambling is legal, a conviction for casino cheating is a felony with some guaranteed penitentiary time. The house doesn't condone cheating among poker players, but unless the cheating jumps up and bites someone in the ass, casino personnel tend to look the other way.

Regardless of whether there is actual cheating (card manipulation or thumbnail deck marking) or merely what I like to call *semi*-cheating (that's the gang-up scam), there are two different ways of handling such situations:

1. *The I'm Gonna Show These Assholes approach.* This is the path taken by Las Vegas–based poker pros and other assorted idiots, the one where you meet the opposition head-on in order to prove that you're someone not to be fucked with. Every time they raise you, you raise back, and every time you have the slightest suspicion that they are bluffing to intimidate, you call. If you suspect any actual cheating you loudly express your fears to the dealer or the poker room manager, and while the noise you make will echo loud and clear for a short while, stooling the cheaters off will, in the long run, be a total waste of your time. If you're in a public casino, then the cheaters will be regulars and you'll be the outsider, so whose word do you think the casino boss is going to take—the everyday regulars' or yours, the guy who's just passing through for the day?

2. *The Full-Blown Pigeon Show* (picture this one as if it stars

Kramer from *Seinfeld*). This is the ploy that works like a charm, though you'll never catch one of the self-imagined sharpies taking this approach, because acting like a pigeon will make the so-called pro appear to be something other than a reincarnation of Nick the Greek and Agent 007 rolled into one. In the Pigeon Show, you merely sit there looking dumb while showing the same reactions as the traveling poker sharpie (reraising the cheaters' raises and calling the cheaters' bluffs), but your demeanor will put across the impression that, instead of a traveling pro and someone not to be fucked with, you're too stupid to fold and therefore you're someone against whom ganging-up tactics are a waste of time.

The difference in results between the two ploys is that whereas in Ploy Number One the other players will knock you off as a professional and therefore keep a watchful eye on you, in Ploy Number Two your opponents will stop ganging up while they play you as someone who doesn't warrant any respect whatsoever, and that's when you should employ some pigeon moves (as outlined in my previous book) in order to take the money home.

Now then. See there, I'm writing my autobiography while I'm doling out poker tips right and left, and, so far, at any rate, this book has been well worth what you paid for it. I'm also dropping little hijacking scenes into the beginning of each chapter, which by the time you finish this book will combine into a riveting description of the event that, once and for all, ended my career as a Big-Time Poker Guy and transformed me into the humble pigeon that I am today.

Keep on readin' on. There's a whole lot here that, as a serious poker player, you'll be able to use.

3

Turning the Tables on the Roundballers

or,
I Discover Tightass Play

Monkey Two "helped" me to my feet by grabbing the zip cuffs that were fastened to my wrists, and yanking my arms upward behind my back as I stood. Sudden tears of pain clouded my vision. I bit my lip to keep from screaming, though I didn't hold back as a show of bravery; I was terrified that any noise I made would cause the shotgun-toting chimp to go ahead and waste me. Throughout the ordeal I expected Monkey One to blow my head off at any second, and I'm sure that the idea crossed his mind.

The initial shock of having a shotgun shoved in my face was wearing off, and in addition to being scared to death I was feeling just a little bit stupid. My game runner/cohort and I had rented a second-floor crib in a garden apartment as the spot to hold our illegal game, and before we'd picked out the right location we'd done a lot of shopping. We needed a place that was relatively easy to find, yet one that had limited access. The two-bedroom that we settled on overlooked a swimming pool, and you reached the entry by climbing one long, metal flight of stairs whose bottom step was at the edge of the parking lot. The rent was higher than that in the surrounding apartments, because our place had exclusive access, but we were glad to pay extra because the from-the-parking-lot-only approach (1) allowed us along with our poker players/customers to come and go unnoticed and (2) gave us a wide-open look at whoever came up the stairs, and therefore plenty of early warning should the cops decide to raid the joint. The law generally became interested in poker games only during election years, but one never knew when the captain might wander into the squad room to find his charges sitting on their asses and order the troops to go out and round up a few gamblers as busywork.

Unfortunately for me, our apartment's location had given Monkey One and Monkey Two the same advantages that had caused us to rent the joint in the first place; the hijackers had managed to tote an arsenal upstairs along with enough zip-cuff material to tie up forty men, and, later, under police questioning, every apartment resident would swear that they'd seen or heard exactly zero. Not only that, these two apes had a bird's-eye view as I tromped up the stairs around four in the afternoon. I'm sure that I had a stupid expression on my face. I'm equally sure that the hijackers felt like laughing out loud when they got a load of me and my stupid expression.

And, oh, yeah. I ignored the metallic clink that I heard.

It wasn't loud, but I heard it distinctly enough so that I should have taken notice. Just as I inserted my key in the lock in preparation for going inside, there was a noise from within the apartment that sounded like two glasses coming together in a toast. In fact, it might've been exactly that—the hijackers' congratulatory toast over picking a victim as dumb as I was. I hesitated and frowned, and right there I should have retreated to the parking lot and waited for the players to arrive so that I could warn them off. I still wonder today what Monkey One and Monkey Two would have done if they'd crouched behind a door inside that empty apartment for several hours, and no one had come in for them to rob.

Would have been a bad day for that pair, but I wasn't smart enough, or attentive enough, to interpret that clinking noise as the only thing that it could have been—someone lurking inside the apartment who was up to no good. Instead, I convinced myself after a few seconds that I'd imagined the noise and blundered on inside.

Actually the sound may have been someone dropping a set of keys; the crime scene folks located no signs of forced entry after the break-in (though, truth be told, law enforcement approached solving the holdup of an illegal poker game with less than boundless enthusiasm), and the hijackers probably had a duplicate key of their own. In fact, the more that I've thought about it over the years, the more certain I am that the apes had a key, and I'm just as certain that I know exactly who provided it for them. But more on that later. I'd gone to the back of the apartment, into the bedroom we'd converted into a poker parlor, and was sitting at the table inventorying our deck supply when Monkey One came up behind me and prodded me with his shotgun.

After Monkey Two had lifted me roughly onto my feet, he motioned me across the hall into the apartment's second bedroom. This bedroom was furnished with two twin beds and also was the one overlooking the swimming pool. Monkey Two told me to lie facedown on the nearest of the beds and also not to look at him. As I put my face to the mattress I was conscious of the shotgun barrel an inch or so behind my left ear. I softly closed my eyes and wondered if that moment was going to be my last one, and if gunfire followed by harp music would be the next two sounds I would hear.

I probably left you with the wrong impression in chapter 2. It's true that just a few months after I lost twenty-five bucks to some basketball stars playing Boo Ray I cleaned those same guys' clocks in a poker game, but that doesn't mean that I morphed from a clueless clod into a card shark in the wink of an eye. I was only a tiny bit better as a poker player during my good-guy-gets-'em-in-the-long-run win than I was as a Boo Ray player on that fateful day when I lost my ass aboard the basketball bus. I'd improved just enough to win against inept competition, and that was about the extent of my progress up to that point.

And while I'm on the subject, I'm eternally grateful for a trait I inherited from my father (though if he knew to what use I've put my gift, he'd kick the lid off his coffin and stalk off in search of me with a razor strap). Daddy was heavily into self-examination from a spiritual standpoint, just as I am in my secular pastime, and though I did win my money back from the student body demigods who'd cheated me out of it, I didn't let minor success go to my head. Even as a high school ninny I was analytical enough to know that the only thing saving me in the poker game was that all three B-ballers were really crappy players— even crappier than I was at the time, and believe me, that's saying a mouthful. The somewhat humbling fact is that even though I clobbered the mental-midget hoopsters, real pros would have doubled over in laughter at the suggestion that I'd become a good poker player by the time I left high school. What remained for me to learn would have filled every shelf at Barnes & Noble and then some.

And, by the way, there is a lesson within a lesson here. I said earlier that the student body heroes had cheated me in the Boo Ray game by passing cards to each other when I wasn't looking, a fact that I learned too late to stop me from paying them. As you go through life as a high-stakes poker player you will occasionally run into cheaters. Some will be so clumsy that they may as well be wearing a sign on their chests, whereas others will be so clever that the only way you'll knock off the scam is by analysis of your results when playing with these folks. Mathematical probabilities are just that—probabilities, not certainties—and while you'll lose with the odds in your favor in honest games at times, whenever the odds *never* win out in the long run against a certain group of players, it's time to decide that the game is not on the square. And that's exactly what caused me to cease all Internet play; I can't prove online cheating but I believe that it exists, and therefore I simply refuse to play.

The existence of cheaters is unfortunate and you can't avoid them entirely, but there is a bright side; the fact that there are cheaters led me to create the following 100 percent accurate Poker Pigeon's Postulate: **Cheaters are terrible players, because if they were any good it wouldn't be necessary for them to cheat.** And the most satisfying thing I've ever learned in poker is how to recognize cheats and take their money in spite of their cheating ways.

But more on cheating in a later chapter. This is the How-I-Learned-to-Play-Poker part of the book, remember? Being a good poker player comes about one step at a time, and I won my money back from the basketball stars only because I figured one thing out while tossing and turning at night worrying about my losses, and even though learning that one little thing didn't make a poker wizard out of me, it was more than enough to baffle the brain trusts of the basketball team.

My initial wee-hours thinking was confined to the game of Boo Ray, naturally, because that's what we played on the basketball bus, but Boo Ray and poker have one thing in common: in either game you have the option of folding your hand after the deal and therefore risk no more than your ante (or your blind in the case of Texas Hold 'Em) in any one hand. And while I strongly believe that it's impossible for a tightass to win in Texas Hold 'Em, just the opposite is true in Boo Ray and most other forms of poker. In fact, in the games that we played in high school, *it was damned near impossible for a tightass to lose!!!*

Listen up, now. It's my primary goal to teach you the difference between a disciplined, rock-solid Hold 'Em player and someone who used to be a winner at other forms of poker, and who blissfully exists a couple of decades behind the times while the good Hold 'Em players make off with his or her bankroll. With the following discussion of the embryonic thoughts that I had in high school, I hereby declare your education officially begun.

As I lay there night after night awash in teen angst over my spilt twenty-five bucks, I pictured the game on the bus where I'd lost my money (I'd yet to find out that I'd been cheated out of my cash, a revelation that, when made, would cause me to begin an entirely different thought process), and it occurred to me that in nearly all of the pots I'd lost, I'd been up against all three hoopsters, and that while I'd waded into every pot during the game just as the other guys had, I'd been the only loser. It took a while, but it finally dawned on me that if I had folded a few hands, I wouldn't have lost nearly as much money.

Yeah, okay, *duh*-uh and all that jazz, but that was really my thought process, as elementary as it sounds. Actually, I don't think my poor showing aboard the basketball bus was any different from most woefully inexperienced card players'; just about every newcomer jumps to the conclusion that if you ain't in the pot there's no way you can win and plays accordingly. After long and serious thought over my loss, I made up my mind that the next time I played Boo Ray, I simply would throw away my hand if it didn't contain at least one cinch winner—the ace of trumps or the king-queen of trumps, or any combination of trumps that would guarantee me at least one trick. About a month later I scraped up enough money to take a seat in another Boo Ray game, this one with some students from another school, and this one with an ante of only a dime. I played for a couple of hours and stuck to my vow of throwing away all hands that didn't contain at least one automatic winner. I won seven bucks and decided that I might be onto something.

A short time later I moved on to poker, high school style,

and my Boo Ray experience gave me a leg up on the other kids going in. Not that I knew poker from Polk salad, but I did have enough sense that when I didn't have shit on the deal, I tossed in my cards. There are no cinch winners in grown-up poker, of course, but that wasn't true in those high school games we played. In those games there actually were a few instances where the first card dealt could guarantee a portion of the pot. It's very true that Mickey Mouse games dealt in high school poker have no more place among hard-eyed gamblin' dudes than a Class A ball club has in Yankee Stadium up against the Bronx Bombers, but rest assured that minor league poker became an important step in my learning process, for reasons that I'll point out as we plod along.

And, by the way, before you turn up your nose at what you're about to read, you may as well come on and fess up. I won't rat you off to "the guys," and a giant Michelob Light won't crush you like in the "men should act like men" commercial, but I'll bet that at one time or another in your life you've played some form of every one of the following games:

Low Hole, High Spade. Us High School Harrys' most popular dealer's choice game, Low Hole, High Spade, is seven-card stud with a few big-time wrinkles. Your lowest hole card is wild along with every other card of the same value that's in your hand (if you have a deuce in the hole, then every other deuce dealt to you becomes wild as well), and to eliminate any chance of you getting screwed on the end by catching a hole card smaller than the wild cards you already have, you're given the option of having the river card dealt to you either faceup or facedown. It's common in this game for two players to tie for high hand with five aces apiece. (This usually causes an argument, because one of the guys nearly always has *six* aces—three real aces along with three wild cards, against the other guy's one ace, one joker, and three wild cards—and will try to argue that six aces beat five, but any moron knows that the best poker hand consists of only five cards. I mean, Jesus Christ, it's not as if Low Hole, High Spade players have thrown *all* of the rules of poker out the window, just most of them.) And not only are the ridiculous number of wild cards in play in Low Hole, High Spade, but the player with the highest spade in the hole gets half the pot. And, oh, yeah, just like all of our high school games, in addition to the low hole cards being wild and whatnot, there's also a joker in the deck that's wild with aces, straights, and flushes. If you've been paying attention, you already know that in keeping with my newfound tightass style of play, unless I had the ace of spades among my original hole cards to guarantee me at least half the pot (or the king of spades if the ace happened to be dealt faceup as the cards came out), I folded after the deal. This used to piss off some of the other players, who got in there and scrambled in every hand, but as long as I kept on winning I wasn't about to change my style.

Jacks, Trips. Five-card draw where you need a pair of jacks or better to open the betting, and where unless a player ends up with three of a kind or better after the cards are all out, the pot remains in the center of the table as a carry-over. Since to pass the deal at that point would rob the next guy of his turn to call the game, the original dealer continues to deal hand after hand until someone finally draws trips or better and wins. My strategy in this game was to fold at the very beginning unless I had three of a kind or better on the first deal, a practice that gave me a lot of downtime, because Jacks, Trips can go on for hours until someone finally wins. I made good use of my time, though; most of our poker games went on in girls' homes where we'd invaded their slumber parties, so after I'd fold my hand I'd go off to the kitchen to talk to the babes and sample the chips and dip until a loud scream from the poker room would tell me that someone had finally drawn three of a kind. During the spring semester of my senior year I gained a lot of weight on the chips and dip and spent a good portion of my winnings on the Friday night dates I'd arrange while the rest of the guys played Jacks, Trips on and on ad nauseum. Although I was never a chick magnet, what I lacked in looks and Steve McQueen charisma I made up for with cash for real restaurant dinners opposed to the drive-in burgers that were the usual fare on dates with the poker losers.

Number Games. Aw, come on, you've played these as well, though admitting it is probably even more humiliating than fessing up to having played Low Hole, High Spade or Jacks, Trips. Those number games really aren't poker. We teenage ninnies played 3/33 and 7/27, and the rules in both were that the player closest to the lower number split the pot with the player closest to the higher number after the cards were all out (and if two or more players had exactly the number, or were the same distance removed from the number, then multiple players tied for both high and low, and the pot was divided five or six ways). In both games, aces count one or eleven the same as in blackjack. In 3/33, face cards count ten and all other cards other than aces count their actual values. In 7/27, faces count one-half a point (yeah, that's what I said), while all other cards except aces count their actual values. Each player gets three cards on the deal, two facedown and one exposed, and in both number games it's possible to have cards that win both high and low (three aces in 3/33, and two aces along with a five in 7/27). After the deal there is a round of betting. Then all players are given the option of taking another card or standing pat. Then there is another round of betting followed by more player card-drawing options, followed by more rounds of betting, and on and on and on until no one wants another card and it becomes showdown time (and don't get the idea that just because players are satisfied with their high hands the game is about to end, because there's always at least one guy who's stood pat all along, representing that he has a low hand, who finally decides that his bluff isn't going to work and suddenly starts drawing cards to try to make a high hand). Christ, talk about slow; number games make Jacks, Trips look like one-card showdown. My strategy in number games was to fold after the deal unless I had cards that put me right on the lower number (or occasionally right on both the high *and* low numbers), and number games provided me even more time in the kitchen with the chips and dips and babes and whatnot.

There were other games that we played, all featuring multiple wild cards, crisscross-patterned community cards on the board (you could use community cards from either the horizontal part of the cross or the perpendicular part, but not both), or tiddles or shucks (both terms mean the same thing, that in some stud games players get to throw away one or more of their cards at the end and get replacements dealt to them, usually after sweetening the pot), but the three games I've just described made up 90 percent of the action, though I could fill hundreds of pages with descriptions of the other far-out games that we played. Basically, our high school poker games were no different from the ones you used to play.

I got my best poker-playing lesson during that period from the father of one of the girls whose slumber parties we liked to invade. This guy had a lot going for him; I never knew how he made his living, but whatever he did it was lucrative. He lived in a one-story house that seemed about two blocks long from end to end, his floors all covered in carpet so plush that you'd sink in up to your ankles. His land sloped from front to back, down to a beautifully wooded creek, and his garage was out back below ground level, right underneath his kitchen. A winding driveway snaked from the street behind the house and up to the entry to the garage. In the garage he kept several vintage cars—a 1902 Oldsmobile one-cylinder was one, and a 1908 REO two-cylinder with a Mother-in-Law seat (sometimes called a rumble seat, especially when Mother-in-Law was listening in) in back was another—in pristine running condition, and the city fathers borrowed those cars every year for their annual turn-of-the-century parade. This guy was no broke, okay?

Even though the astonishing one-story length of his home afforded him the luxury of keeping us loud obnoxious teenagers as far away from his bedroom as possible, the guy didn't always take advantage of his chance for quiet and sometimes got about three sheets to the wind and came in to crash our party and invade our poker game. He was the shark of the weekly rich guys' game at the country club (in fact, I ran into him about ten years later when a couple of us pros managed an invite into that very game, and on that occasion he spent a long evening looking at me and scratching his head, trying to figure out where he'd seen me before, as we plundered him and his friends for a couple grand) and had been picking all those lawyers' and bankers' pockets for years. The guy certainly didn't need what cash he could win off of us high schoolers. I believe to this day that he had no interest in our silly wild-card games and only muscled his way into the teenager party in order to make sure nobody felt up his little girl while he was at the other end of the house snoring away. Around ten P.M., when the party would be heating up and the poker game would be under way, in he'd stagger with whiskey on his breath and a roll of bills in his pocket and flop down in an empty seat. I don't understand how he could possibly see his cards at times, his eyes were so bloodshot, but you know what? Every time he played, he won. Often he and I would be the only winners in the game, and all I can remember about his play is that, drunk or not, he folded just as many hands as I did.

Anyway, one night after I'd folded a hand of Jacks, Trips or one of the number games and had gone into the kitchen for some babe conversation and whatnot, I bumped into Host Girl's Father at the chips and dips table. Actually, I didn't bump into him; he *stumbled* into me, breathing bourbon in my face and smearing the front of my jeans with onion and chive dip. He pointed a quivering finger at my chest and slurred, "You've played some poker before, aintcha?"

Actually, I had only recently taken up the game after my Boo Ray experience on the basketball bus had caused me to discover the tightass plan of attack. But, in full teenager-wanting-to-be-taken-seriously mode, I said, "Well, yeah, a little here and there," and tried to slant my look to seem really mysterious and in and with-it.

"I knew it," he said. "I can tell." Then he moved in closer and, as I nearly gagged on the alcohol fumes, said, "Those kids playing all them wild cards, a real poker player can beat them at their own game."

I was too busy feeling proud of myself to really think through what he said, but later on I had the time and remember his words as if he'd spoken them yesterday. It's true that a tightass (which was obviously Host Girl's Father's definition of a good poker player) can beat a lot of really poor poker players at some really Mickey Mouse poker games merely by folding his or her cards unless he or she has a cinch winner, but a good *Hold 'Em* player is a completely different animal. In fact, if learning the difference between a real Hold 'Em player and a mere tightass is the only thing you get out of this book, your money will be well spent. As you kick your motor into learning gear, look for me to preach tight but aggressive in each and every chapter. Tight-but-aggressive Hold 'Em players take the money home, while tightasses watch their money slowly circle the bowl as they scratch their heads in bewilderment.

For example, no one really knows where wild cards originated, or who first thought of having high spades in the hole split pots, but I happen to have a theory on both inventions just as I have a theory about all things poker, and the further I plod along through life the more I believe that my theories are right on target. I think that some poker hustler dreamed up wild cards so that inexperienced players, believing that with so many wild cards in play they were gonna make good hands just about every time, would play in every pot while the hustler would sit back and wait for something choice before he would risk a nickel. I know that's the way it worked in our high school games; normally I was the only player who regularly folded (unless Host Girl's Father was in the game) while the others stuck nearly every pot out to the bitter end (occasionally guys would fold when they got a phone call or received an invitation from some girl to go out to the car for a little hanky-panky, but otherwise they were in every pot, firing away, and since Host Girl's Father's regular presence kept hanky-panky with the babes down to a minimum, us two tightasses were always in for plenty of loose donations from the boys).

And as for the high spade in the hole splitting the pot, well, I believe the origin of that game to be quite a bit more sinister than the invention of wild cards. If we could find a way to do the proper historical research, I'd bet decent bucks that cheats invented seven-card stud poker games where the high spade in the hole took half the pot. A situation where there is only one card—the ace of spades in this instance—to palm or maneuver to the bottom of the deck, where the cheat can easily slip it to himself or his cohorts, is the professional cheater's dream. Other cheating ploys involve manipulating too many cards for the cheater to be certain that he won't get caught, and old-time cheats had to be ready to make a dash for the exit or reach for their shootin' irons whenever one of the other players barked, "Hold it, there," during the cheater's deal. When some road gambler invented the game where the high spade in the hole split the pot, he no doubt saved his own life along with many of his fellow cheaters'.

So them's my off-the-top-of-the-head opinions as to the Mickey Mouse games' origin, but really, the only things you need to remember about wild cards and high spades splitting pots is that wild cards throw all poker odds out the window, and that any time you sit in a game where the high spade in the hole splits the pot, be sure to cut the cards often and watch the dealer like a hawk. A tightass is a sure winner in such games just about every time he sits down—and if the tightass knows what he's doing, he'll win no matter how many cheats are involved—so if you have no desire to improve your skills past the tightass level, and you want to spend the rest of your life muscling your way into high school games, then that's the path you should take. At some point, though—at least by the time you reach forty—you will become the target of irate parents sick of you robbing their kids of their allowances, and the molestation cops will be watching you as if you were a priest turned loose on a playground. Like everything else in life, you gotta grow up in poker or be left by the wayside.

But during my senior semester in high school, and for a few years thereafter, I thought that being a tightass would guarantee that I'd be a winner at the poker table clear on into the next century. I became complacent—okay, maybe complacent isn't a strong enough word; I got so fat and happy that my play became sloppy as hell—because I was winning more money than I'd ever dreamed of winning, and I was headed into my sophomore year in college before I saw any reason to improve my skills. I've always subscribed to the if-it-ain't-broke-don't-fix-it theory, and the theory works in most cases, but not where poker is concerned. As I was to find out the hard way, you must learn as you go or lose any edge that you might think you have.

Just remember: **A tightass cannot win in Hold 'Em, and failure to recognize that fact has cost many aspiring poker players big bucks, not to mention having shortcircuited many promising gambling careers before they were under way.**

Why can't a tightass win in Texas Hold 'Em? Because in the Mickey Mouse high school games I've described, the tightass can sit back and wait for cinch winners on the deal; in Hold 'Em, however, cinch winners on the deal don't exist. Two aces is the best starting hand possible, of course, but two aces only go to a player once every 160-some-odd hands on average. If you folded every combination other than two aces, in a fifteen-and-thirty limit game you would have spent $320 in forced bets (sixteen times around the table in a ten-handed game times the twenty bucks in forced bets required to get you around the table once) for every pair of pocket rockets you picked up, so you'd have to win $320 on average each time you played in a hand *just to break even*. In our old high school games only the dealer anted, so the tightass could afford to sit there like a stone until he found the ace of spades in the hole, or a hand where he had a total of either three or seven, depending on the number game, on the opening deal.

And as for the other "big" Hold 'Em hands such as AK, although AK is a *statistical* favorite over nearly all other two-card combinations, I personally believe that AK is the most overrated hand in Hold 'Em, and that weak players waste more money raising before the flop with AK than they'll ever win with the hand. Later on we'll get into a discussion of how big unpaired two-card hands should be played, but for now just let this chapter's lesson sink in:

Since Texas Hold 'Em is about the only poker game being played at high levels today, and therefore is the only game worth learning, if you're unable to adjust your style of play from the tightass methods that have stood you well in other games, then you should give up poker altogether because you will never be a winner at Hold 'Em. Loosening up will require a bigger bankroll than you're used to bringing to the games, because you're going to be seeing many more flops than a tightass would ever dare to, which means it will take longer for skillful play to pull you through. Coming up with more risk capital isn't always easy for a poker player, but a bigger bankroll, say twice the amount you used to bring along when you were groveling around as a tightass, is mandatory. Playing tight-but-aggressive Hold 'Em will put you in a big hole at times, especially when the draw-out flea jumps off your ass and bites the other guys, but if you keep your cool you can recover. Remember, if you can't stand the heat that looser play is going to put on you, you ought to forget poker and get the hell our of the kitchen.

And with that mouthful said, we're now ready to progress past my high school memories. The next chapter is a doozy. In it I'm going to tell you about my college years, and about the series of happenings that changed me from a square-john college guy with a business future into a forty-year veteran pilgrim in the poker world. In climbing to the next level, we'll dispense with the wild cards and number games, and although we'll develop a (slightly) more sophisticated style of play than we've been using, we'll still be nowhere near the point where a real pro is going to think that our poker is anything but laughable. We are, however, merrily on our way.

4

Frat Rats and Other Suckers

or,
The Phi Delts Keep Me in Booze and Babes

I don't know when Monkey Two took his shotgun and left the room, but he'd been gone for a while before I realized that he was gone. He'd told me not to look at him and, picturing those twin barrels an inch or so behind my ear, I lay there with my nose to the mattress and my eyes squinched closed, still as a statue. What might have been five minutes—or for all I know an hour—later, I mumbled something like, "Look, I'm hurting. Can I turn on my side?" No one answered and I heard no movement behind me. After asking the question again and not getting an answer, I took a deep breath and turned my head around.

I was alone in the bedroom.

Man, that Monkey One and Monkey Two. What a couple of kidders. One surprise after another with those guys.

It didn't take a genius to figure out where Monkey Two had headed. He'd gone to meet with Monkey One, and both hijackers would now be crouched inside the front door lying in wait for the players as they straggled up the stairs looking for action. Each player,

*after ringing the doorbell, would find a gun jammed in his face
and his hands zipcuffed behind. As if in answer to my thoughts,
the doorbell chimed in the distance.*

*I decided that the guntoters wouldn't shoot anyone as long as
we didn't give them any trouble. I'd never been through a poker
game hijacking, but I knew plenty of men who had, and I'd never
heard of anyone being killed during such a robbery.*

But there's always a first time, right?

Just keep your cool, *I thought,* and you'll get through this.
Money's always replaceable. Give them whatever they want, and
everything will be fine.

I hoped.

*I began to worry about one of our regular players, a retired
heavyweight who didn't take shit from anybody—and who, in fact,
had once broken Joe Frazier's jaw in a setup exhibition where he
was supposed to be Frazier's punching bag. If anybody might challenge the hijackers and get us all killed in the process, this boxer
was the guy. But he'd been short of money lately, and just yesterday he'd told me to count him out of the game until he could raise
another stake. I sighed in relief; other than the boxer, there weren't
any players who wouldn't cooperate with two armed monkeys. Our
players would be meek as lambs. Even if my partner and I had to
make up the individuals' losses out of our own pockets, that solu-
tion would be better than having someone shot. If I'd just take it
easy, this would all be over before I knew it.*

*And just as I was getting into a better frame of mind, Mon-
key Two came in the bedroom with his shotgun leveled on none other
than the boxer, the boxer's hands in the air, his expression furious.
The boxer wore shorts and a T-shirt, his muscles pumped as if he'd
just left the gym. Monkey Two used the zip cuffs to tie the boxer's
hands behind him and told him to lie down next to me. He then
told us both not to make a sound and left the room once more.*

As soon as Monkey Two left, the boxer scooted around on the bed until he was sitting up with his back to me. "Work on these cuffs," he said. "Get me loose, and I can take both of those guys."

"I, uh, thought you weren't coming today," I croaked.

"I borrowed some money," he said. "Hurry up. When that sonofabitch comes back I'm jamming that shotgun up his ass. I'll teach 'em not to fuck with buddies of mine."

I closed my eyes as my heart thumped like a big bass drum, trying like hell to tear its way through my breastbone.

I don't care if you're a poker bum or a corporate CEO, I'll lay odds that you can point to an exact moment when your life's direction changed. Maybe it was your marriage or the birth of your first child. Or it might have been a change in decisions as to where you wanted to live, or a choice you made between different job offers. Or—and poker bums are big on this one—it might've been the *loss* of a job (getting fired for sleeping on the job, because you stayed out all night, in other words) followed by a decision to suck it up and live by your wits from then on.

I had not one but two life-changing moments on my first day in college, and if it hadn't been for Incident Number One, Incident Number Two never would have happened. I'd been to the first meeting of all my classes that morning (which would soon become a rarity, me attending all my classes on any given day) and, freshman beanie perched on top of my head, I timidly approached the student union, looking right and left, terrified that some upperclassman would confront me and make me do push-ups or eat raw eggs or shit in my hat or something. As I mounted the first step, someone tapped me on the shoulder from behind. I swallowed hard and turned around.

The shoulder tapper was a guy that I knew, though knowing him didn't make things any more comfortable for me. He had gone to my own high school and had graduated a year before me, so now he was a dreaded college sophomore. Sophomores, having just shed their own fish status over the summer, were always the worst freshmen baiters, and while having acquaintances among the upperclassmen worked to a fish's advantage on occasion, at other times knowing upperclassmen could mean harassment above and beyond, depending on what the fish's prior relationship to the tormentor happened to be. I knew one fish who'd two-timed a girl back in high school. Like the guy tapping me on the shoulder, the girl had graduated a year ahead of us and had gone on to college, and, on finding out that her former cheating boyfriend had enrolled as a freshman, had made him sing "Short People" while standing in front of the women's dorm with his pants down around his ankles. The guy who'd just tapped me on the shoulder had lived only a couple of blocks away from my house when we were growing up, and though I didn't know him very well, I seemed to recall shooting him the finger as he stood in his yard while I drove by with a carload of guys egging me on. I held my breath and hoped that the shoulder tapper didn't remember that incident.

The shoulder tapper put his nose an inch from mine. "Where you going, *freshman*?" he said.

His tone didn't forecast good things in store for me. I answered as required. "*Sir*. I'm going to the student union, *sir*."

"No, you're not. You're going to report to the football stadium."

I pictured me running laps until someone had to call for an ambulance. "*Sir*. Can I stop at the dorm and put on shorts, *sir*?"

"What the hell for?"

"*Sir*, if I'm going to run laps . . ."

"You're not going to run laps, freshman. You're going to report as my assistant student manager of the football team."

"*Sir*. Yes, *sir*. Right away, *sir*." Before the guy could change his mind, I double-timed it toward the stadium, the grandstands towering over the campus in the distance, as relief flooded over me.

As I hustled along I was thinking, *Oh, wow, assistant football manager, team trips and hanging with the guys and whatnot!* I was *pumped*, no doubt about it, but if I could've forecast the future I would've seen that my college career would have fared better academically if my old high school compadre had made me give him a hundred push-ups. He was the head student football manager and knew that I'd been the basketball players' jock strap washer/sweat wiper-offer in high school, so I was the obvious choice when the coach told the guy to find himself a freshman assistant. So for once an upperclassman had stopped a freshman on campus with no punishment in mind—though, I suspect, due to all of the disgusting stuff the guy had me do as his assistant that fall, he also remembered the time in high school that I gave him the finger.

By now you're probably wondering how becoming assistant football manager in college was a life-changing moment or, more importantly, how this story has diddly to do with helping you improve your poker, but remember that everything comes in stages and that I've already told you there were two incidents that day and that one led to another. I actually went to college with good intentions, a future as a lawyer or business consultant uppermost on my mind, and I had been to all my classes on that first day and had taken notes and all of that happy bullshit. Though I'd won quite a bit of money off the basketball morons and their cohorts during my last high school semester, a future at the poker table had never even remotely occurred to me, but becoming assistant football manager completely changed my direction as a student. As the assistant football manager, instead of having business majors and art students and drama students and whatnot as my associates, my circle of friends became restricted to a bunch of football jocks, and football jocks and their skewed slants on life became the extent of my social education. Football jocks believe (and the public reinforces this belief) that the rest of humanity is there merely to fall at their feet and worship them. Their interests extend to playing football, getting drunk, and trying to screw every coed on campus, and from that day forward I did my damnedest to fit into that group and embrace the jockstrap way of life, even though my own athletic ability stopped at getting out of bed without falling on my ass and tying my own shoelaces with no assistance. So, *poof!*—there went my future as a brilliant student and a future lawyer, and I'd only been in college for half a day.

The second life-altering incident occurred on that same fateful day, while I was rubbing a guy's ass in the training room.

Now hold on. I'm not sure I like the way that statement might sound. I wasn't *affectionately or sensuously* rubbing his ass, and I sure as hell didn't grope him from the front after I got his ass in my hands. My first day at football practice, after I'd nearly broken my back hauling around tackling dummies and shoulder pads and crap, the team thundered into the locker room when the workout was over. I went about putting equipment away and hoped that in my state of exhaustion I could make it into bed that night. But lo and behold, my day was far from finished. The team's star running back/pass receiver—and a guy who later survived ten seasons in the NFL and played in a Super Bowl—had pulled a glute, and the head trainer had ordered the head student manager to give the guy an ultrasonic treatment. The head student manager—the same guy whom I'd given the finger to in high school—understandably didn't want to fool with the football player's ass, so he delegated the duty to me. I tried not to look at the player as he climbed up on the training table, but eventually I had to. And there, right under my nose, was his snow-white ass, gleaming in the light from above.

I don't believe that ultrasonic treatment heals anything that wouldn't take care of itself over time, and my training room experience convinced me that the treatment's real purpose is to force a lot of student trainers and managers to massage a lot of football players' asses, though the people who sell the equipment have the athletic world believing that ultrasound is the next-best healing process to Jesus laying hands on the leper colony. The machine itself is a squatty arrangement with a cord sprouting from the top, and at the end of the cord is a gizmo that looks like a rock 'n' roller's handheld microphone. In treating sore asses you first pour a clear, really slick oil (I'm not kidding, this goop looks exactly like baby oil, and you feel as if you oughtta be saying, "Make you feel *good*, baby," as you uncap the bottle) on whichever ass cheek has the alleged pulled muscle (in this case it was the left one), turn on the machine, and then massage the ass with the microphone-looking gizmo, spreading the oil around on the guy's ass until the jockstrap decides that he's had enough. Some jocks feel about as dumb as the guy who's rubbing his ass with the ultrasonic wand, and therefore want the ordeal over with in a hurry, whereas others seem to enjoy the treatment and lay there with their asses exposed and their eyes closed in rapture, on and on and on into the night.

Oh, yeah. This is supposed to be a book about playing poker, isn't it? So okay, what follows is the poker connection.

As I stood there rubbing the wand around in the oil I'd spread on the guy's ass, the team's starting quarterback came over and stood there watching. I fixated on the ceiling and whistled aimlessly, scared to death that the quarterback would want his own ass rubbed when I'd finished with the other guy's. Instead, the quarterback leaned over the running back/receiver; stage-whispered, "Might be some fresh meat"; and jerked his head in my direction.

Now I *really* concentrated on the ceiling and rubbed the wand around in the oil faster and faster. I didn't want to be fresh meat. I wanted the hell out of there.

The guy on the table turned his head and said to me out of the side of his mouth, "Freshman, do you play poker?"

I couldn't believe my ears. I glanced at the quarterback, who watched me as if I were a slice of moist barbecued chicken. I said, "I have played some, *sir*."

The guy who was getting his ass rubbed now turned on his side and took the wand from me. "You don't gotta call me 'sir.' What you gotta do is show up in the dorm attic thirty minutes after practice. We play poker every night up there, some nights all night. What you gotta do is bring money, and we're gonna save you a seat."

"I'll be there, *sir*," I croaked.

Now the quarterback spoke up. "I'm gonna tell you, freshman, if you want in you're in, but this ain't no high school poker game. This is the real thing. No wild cards when it's your deal, and no funny-assed games. This here is sure 'nough poker, got that?"

I assured the two jocks that I had the picture and that they were coming in loud and clear, and that they wouldn't see anything out of me but real, adult-type poker play. I'm not sure if they believed me—and I'm not sure if I knew what sort of sure 'nough poker they were talking about—but at least the running back now had an incentive to end the ass-rubbing session and make tracks for the poker game. He got up from the table and strolled off toward the shower with a towel draped over his shoulder. He wasn't limping or even wincing. Christ, to this very day I'm not even sure that there was anything wrong with the guy's ass, and I suspect that he just wanted out of practice for a few days and was faking an injury. I put the equipment away in record time and dashed off for the student center dining hall. Just a half hour earlier I'd been so pooped that I wasn't sure if I could drag myself into bed, but now adrenaline had me wired. Man, was I ever ready to play some cards.

I raced through the chow line, wolfed down a plate of food so quickly that I didn't taste a single morsel (which wasn't always a bad thing in the school cafeteria, not being able to taste the food), ran over to the athletic dorm, and hustled up the stairs to the attic. There was a lot of useless crap in the attic—broken beds, busted chairs, even a cracked toilet sitting in the corner—and toward the far end of the room a single lightbulb glowed from the ceiling. Underneath the light sat a bunch of Me Hongry–type athletes, some wearing shirts and some naked from the waist up, their massive shoulders hunched as they squinted at their cards, the whole scenario playing out under a fog of cigarette smoke that created a sort of "Hound of the Baskervilles" surreality. Everybody smoked in those days, and I mean *everybody*, including me, but to see all of those guys puffing away in the athletic dorm with football season just around the corner was a bit of a shock. Coke bottles half filled with water served as ashtrays, and there was an occasional hissing sound whenever someone snuffed out a butt by dropping it in the water. One guy had a package of Beechnut chewing tobacco in his shirt pocket, his jaw full of cud as he spat into an empty Coke bottle. I walked timidly over and had a look. Right in front of me, those six man-mountain football players were involved in the weirdest-looking poker game that I've ever seen. Before or since. Bar none.

Actually, the parts when taken individually weren't all that strange, but the whole was something out of *Alice in Wonderland*. First there was the deck of cards—blue Bicycle Rider Backs. Some of the cards were limp and dog-eared but others were slick and almost new. I looked over one guy's shoulder at his hand, and at first I couldn't figure out what he was doing. The game was obviously five-card draw, and the jock in question held in one hamlike paw four clubs and a single heart, yet when it came his turn to act, the bastard *raised*. I scratched my head and squinted for a closer look, and on examination I understood what was happening here. The guy did have a flush-busting seven of hearts—this was one of the new-looking cards in the deck—in his mitt, but someone had taken a pen and marked through the sevens in the opposite corners and underneath the numbers had written "10 of clubs." So obviously the boys had a deck with some cards missing and had combined their deck with a second deck that was also short of cards until the number totaled the necessary fifty-three counting the joker. Neither deck had contained a ten of clubs, so the guys had improvised and gone to work with a ballpoint. I wondered how many cards had been altered to make up a deck. As I thought that one over, someone called the guy's bet, he rolled over his hand to announce a flush, and he swept in the pot. I did notice that the pot seemed awfully small in relation to the number of players, and I vaguely wondered why, but I was so intrigued with the makeshift deck that it would take a while for the answer to dawn on me.

And, oh, yeah, there was one other little thing that didn't occur to me at the time. I was about to play poker with a bunch of guys who couldn't afford a new deck of cards.

I did snap to to one thing immediately, however. With the newer cards mixed in with the dog-eared, limp cards, it should be easy to memorize which cards were among the newer ones, and although it would be impossible to tell the *exact* card in a player's hand by its newness or dog-earedness, it would be a piece of cake to *eliminate* certain cards from the player's possible hand, and whoever took the time to memorize the newer cards would have one helluvan advantage. But hold it, the little angel on my shoulder said, would memorizing the newer cards be cheating? To this day I think the answer to that one is somewhere in a gray area, but—and I especially believe this next part after getting to know all of the players in the jockstrap game— anyone in the game who *didn't* know the newer cards by heart would be a fool.

So much for the deck. The chips were cheap cardboard in three colors, and some of the chips were split in half so that one side was red, blue, or white, and the other side was grayish paper. Later I'd learn that there were players in the game who'd use their thumbnails to intentionally split their chips, thus doubling their stacks without winning a single hand. And if you think this habit played havoc with whoever was banking the game when it came cash-in time, you're wrong. I'll get to the payout to the winners in another page or two.

An unwieldy piece of fiberboard, about seven by seven, served as a table while two packing crates standing on end formed the base. The playing surface sagged on the sides, and the players made do with trunks, boxes, and even one three-seater church pew as chairs and propped the weak portions of the table up on their knees. The game had an audience, more football jocks crowded around peering over shoulders at the players' hands, whispering among themselves. The table talk was different from that in any poker game I've ever seen; whereas in most games the players talk previously played hands and odds of making this hand or that hand, all these guys seemed to care about was football—which player could run the fastest and who would hit the hardest and who was a badass and who was a chickenshit on the gridiron. I remember that one guy tried to describe the knockers on this coed he'd stripped naked one night, but the other jocks weren't even interested *in that bit of information* and quickly returned the topic to football and the merits of knocking people's asses off from the blind side.

Did I mention that there was room at the table for seven, and that only six were seated? Or that ten or twelve guys were standing around, yet no one wanted the empty seat? As I walked over, the sore-assed running back—currently sitting on his ultrasonic ass and showing no pain—looked up, grinned, and patted the space next to him. "Got a seat for you, freshman." The other man-mountains grinned as one.

It sure wasn't the last time that I'd be pegged as the pigeon, but I don't think my role has ever been quite so obvious. I sat on the box beside the running back and pulled out a twenty-dollar bill. One of the giants snatched the money, counted out chips, and pushed a stack over in front of me.

It was my running back/buddy's deal. He gathered in the cards, some of which were so dog-eared that they bent even more as he shuffled. He looked at me. "Remember, freshman. No wild cards. No kid games."

"I've got you, *sir*," I said timidly.

"Great. This is dealer's choice, and now we're gonna play 'Eat Your Wallet.' "

Christ, I had to be hearing things. I said, "Eat your what?"

"Wallet. Look, you ain't never played any adult poker, so we're gonna explain it one time. After that, freshman, you're on your own. This game is five-card draw, high-low split."

"But what's the 'Eat your—"

"I ain't finished. After your draw you're gonna put your hand facedown, and we're gonna roll them over one at a time, like stud. There's a bet after every rollover. High card bets, always. After the cards are all out, the high hand takes half and the low hand takes half. You got that?"

"I think I can—"

"I ain't finished, freshman. After you roll four cards up and got one left in the hole, then you can tiddle."

I'm sure I looked as confused as any first-year calculus student. "Tiddle?"

"Shuck. Throw one card away and get another one. That's the game. Don't ask no more questions. Money talks and bull-shit walks in this game, pal."

Jesus, I thought. *Say what?* I wanted to ask him to explain the game one more time, but he was giving me a hard-eyed look, so I didn't. What I did was, I picked up my hand when he dealt it to me, noted that I had neither a pat wheel (perfect low and a cinch winner) nor a pat full house, so I folded. The hand took what seemed like half an hour to play. I longed for the slumber party games, where I could wander around and visit with the babes.

And the game called Eat Your Wallet was only the beginning. As the deal progressed around the table, the games got more and more creative. I won't bother you with a descriptive list, but, suffice it to say, the game called Eat Your Wallet was the tamest of all. We were up to here with community cards (in crisscross patterns, circular patterns, or whatever pattern you can think of), High Chicago (this was the high spade in the hole splitting the pot just like in my high school game, only in "grown-up poker" there weren't any wild cards), Low Chicago (yeah, you've got it, lowball where the *low* spade in the hole split the pot), roll your own, spit in the . . . Oh, hell, I think you've got the idea.

I reverted to the only winning poker strategy that I knew, and in full tightass mode I must have folded twenty hands in a row until one of the guys, a lineman who looked as if he had a ten-pound-a-day raw meat habit, said, "You ain't playing many hands, *freshman.* You oughtta get your feet wet." After that I called a few bets to make it look good, not to mention to avoid the possibility of a country ass kicking from Raw Meat.

Finally, I picked up the ace of spades in a hand of High Chicago, and here my real indoctrination into college poker jockstrap style began. I was a cinch to capture half the pot, but since this was a new environment for me, I wasn't sure how to bet. If it had been my old high school game I would've let the hammer down and would've launched into betting and raising, full speed ahead. But in the old childish high school poker game no one ever folded no matter how much was bet, and I assumed that since these were more mature college guys I should slow play it, letting whoever had the high hand drive the action, possibly until I could get a raise or two in when the cards were all out. And so I slow played it, checking and calling until the final facedown card hit the table, and then managed a couple of raises on the end. I remember as clearly as if it were yesterday that Raw Meat caught two consecutive diamonds to make a flush, drawing out on the sore-assed running back's three of a kind. I showed my spade, and then Raw Meat and I got ready to split the pot.

But, lo and behold and Christ Almighty, there wasn't any pot to split. At least not to speak of; there were four or five red chips and maybe one blue in the center of the table, no more than that, and with the amount of action there'd been in the hand there should've been at least ten times as much in the pot as there actually was.

I looked helplessly across the table at Raw Meat and shrugged my shoulders.

Raw Meat seemed puzzled. He frowned at the four or five chips in the pot, and then understanding spread slowly across his face (you'd just have to have been there; picture Wile E. Coyote's expression as he realizes that the roadrunner has just put another one over on him, and that the ol' coyote's hat is about to explode one more time). Finally, Raw Meat said, "You assholes come across with your lights, you hear me?"

Until that day I'd never played in a poker game where players drew light, and in case you never have, it works this way. If a player doesn't have enough chips in front of him to call a bet, he pulls the amount of the bet out of the pot, sets it in front of him, and continues to draw more lights until he either folds or the hand is over. Once the hand is complete, the player drawing light is supposed to match his lights with real money and shove both the lights and the cash into the pot, but as I was about to find out, in the jockstrap poker game things seldom worked out the way they were supposed to when it came to the cash in the pot or in the till.

Raw Meat, bless his heart, had alerted me to a local quirk in the game, so now I mentally took inventory. There were stacks of lights in front of every participant except for me and (I thought at the time) Raw Meat, and during the last round of betting, each time I'd tossed a bet into the pot, *four* players had drawn light to call me so that chips were *coming out* of the pot at four times the rate at which they were going in; hence, there was next to nothing left when it came to divvy-up time. The stacks of lights just sat there in front of the players, who looked at the ceiling and whistled an unknown tune. No one made a move to go in his pocket for the matching cash.

And guess what. No one was going to.

I suppose that if my brawn-before-brains newest best friend—Raw Meat—hadn't brought up the subject, the guys would have surreptitiously kept their lights and commenced playing with the held-out chips as if they'd suddenly found money growing on a vine. Today, any time I sit down in a new (to me) poker game, I watch the other players very closely, both for mannerisms that I think might help me in pots against them and for anything that I might suspect as cheating, but keep in mind that at the time I wandered into the jockstrap game I was a virgin, fresh from high school. To be fair to modern poker, I seldom notice anything out of the ordinary anymore in games where I'm playing, especially since 90 percent of the poker I play goes on in legal card rooms. But I have detected cheaters in the past and have the college jockstrap game to thank for my vigilance. Thank God the stakes weren't all that high in the athletic dorm game, though it seemed like a fortune at the time.

Thanks, old footballers. I loved you guys back then, lose or tie, and still think of you fondly every time I get mixed up in a crooked poker game.

Oh, and as for the reaction at the table when Raw Meat demanded that the players account for their lights? You're probably not going to believe this, but please trust me that the following
is a dead-on account. Think about it this way: I couldn't make
this story up if I wanted to.

First, there was a sheepish downward look by each of the
lights holder-outers, followed by innocent grins. Then the sore-
assed running back—who'd held out the biggest of the four
stacks of lights—said, "Oh, sure." Then he tossed his lights into
the center of the table in a jumbled pile.

The other three holdouts followed suit until there was a fair-
sized amount in the pot. Raw Meat nodded, drug the pot, and
then started to divide the chips into equal stacks, one for him
and one for me.

I'm sure that my mouth was open like a flytrap. Christ, Raw
Meat was even dumber than he looked, and believe me, that's
saying a mouthful. So the guys had given up their lights. So what?
They were supposed to *match their lights with hard cash*. My winner's share of the profits had improved when the holdouts had
sent their lights sliding into the pot, but the pot was still only
about half the size that it should have been.

I started to say something, then paused. I was looking at the
stack of chips in front of my pot-divvying buddy. Not the equal
one-for-you and one-for-me piles that Raw Meat was creating,
but the three-inch stack between his massive elbows. That stack
was in all three colors, the colors in no particular order. They
were the only chips he'd had when the hand was finished.

I now understood why Raw Meat hadn't told the holdouts
to match their lights with cash, and the answer had nothing to
do with his stupidity. Raw Meat himself had drawn light in the
pot, and he was making such a show of dividing the pot into
two exactly equal amounts *because he intended to keep his own
lights and add them to his stack* and was hoping that if he made

enough of a show out of keeping the others honest, I wouldn't notice that his own stack was bigger than it should have been.

I had a choice to make. A real man would've stood up for himself and demanded that the others match their lights, and that Raw Meat surrender his holdout money and match it as well.

Raw Meat had hands like hams, arms like tree trunks, and a permanent snarl on his face. A couple of the other poker players were even bigger than Raw Meat.

Stand up for myself? Get up in a bunch of guys' faces, any one of who could break me in half? I mentally weighed my options.

Finally, I swallowed hard and said to Raw Meat, "Uh, you weren't light in that pot, were you?"

He froze with a blue chip in each hand, ready to place them on separate equal stacks. He looked at me and scowled.

I eye measured the distance to the exit and tensed my knees, ready to leap to my feet in case I had to make a run for it.

Raw Meat slowly grinned. He looked down at the stack of lights in front of him as if he'd never seen them before. "I plumb forgot," he said, then shoved his lights into the center of the table and began to divide them into equal piles.

Actually, all of Raw Meat's lights should have gone to me, and I debated about calling him down on that point. Finally, I decided that a half-full glass was better than an empty one, kept my mouth shut, and let myself be screwed. When Raw Meat finally gave me my share of the pot, I counted to find that I'd collected about half of what I'd actually won.

And I hadn't seen anything yet.

I was sort of between a rock and a hard place for the rest of that session, because I sure didn't want to tick off a bunch of guys who'd be throwing sweaty jerseys in my direction for months and years to come (not to mention that the celebrity factor came into play; remember, these were major college football players whose names and pictures appeared in the paper on a daily basis, and just a few months earlier I'd been in high school and some of these guys' action photos had hung on the wall in my bedroom), but, at the same time, I couldn't just let this blatant den of thieves make off with my entire bankroll. As the game went on into the wee small hours I retreated into full-blown tightass mode and participated in only two or three more pots. Since I won at least half of every pot in which I played, I came out substantially ahead, even though I took in only about half of what I should have because of the situation with the guys drawing light. Actually, I came out better than a lot of the other pot winners, because each time I won or split a pot my first act was to scan the table for lights to make sure that while not a single light was ever matched with cash, at least the lights went back into the pot, where they belonged. Other guys who won pots weren't nearly so vigilant, and as a result, several guys not only failed to match their lights, but they simply *kept* their lights and continued to play on them.

Around one in the morning, realization hit me square between the eyes. No one really likes to play with cheaters, but even though this was the weirdest card game outside of the Mad Hatter's merry unbirthday party, I decided to grin and bear it, because *as long as I played in tightass mode it was going to be impossible for me to lose.* The jockstraps' cheating didn't involve any card manipulation of the kind I was to see in later years, only some very clumsy guys holding out their lights, *and these guys were such lousy poker players that even if I collected only half of what I won, I'd still show a tidy profit, just as I had in the games back in high school.* In all the time that I sat there I recall only one other player who ever folded his hand, a calm-eyed slim athletic type who sat across from me and watched the goings-on with detached amusement. In that session he and I were the only winners, and later on this same guy would become my guide into the real, live poker world. But more on him later. We haven't quite left the merry unbirthday party, college jockstrap style, though we are about to.

I congratulated myself for discovering a money tree in the attic of the athletic dorm right up to the moment that the game broke up and it was time to cash in. My indoctrination into sure 'nough grown-up poker had come and gone and I was none the worse for wear. I sorted my chips into even stacks, shoved the chips to the jockstrap who was acting as banker, and sat back and waited to be paid.

Little did I know.

Not only did I not collect my winnings, but I didn't even get all of the twenty bucks I'd used to buy in. The calm-eyed customer and I were the only winners, and actually he'd won a little more than I had. He'd bought into the game for ten dollars. There was thirty dollars, total, in the bank, my twenty and his ten, and, it turned out, *everyone else in the game had played on credit.* In a diplomatic move, the banker (the same guy whose ass I'd been rubbing in the training room) decided to divide the cash equally between the two winners, fifteen dollars apiece, so the end result was a five-dollar profit for the calm-eyed guy and a five-dollar loss for yours truly. For the rest of our winnings we got scribbled IOUs. I didn't even read the small squares of paper at first, and when I finally did examine them when alone in my room, *I couldn't make out a single signature.* Years have dimmed my memory—not to mention that I'd just as soon forget that day altogether—but I think as the school year plodded on I collected about half the IOUs. Any time one of the jocks paid me any portion of what he owed, it was a shock, because even though I never would've admitted it, *I didn't have the slightest idea who owed me, or how much any one individual owed.*

So, okay, it's now time for you to laugh in my face. I'd messed up big-time, though after all these years I still don't believe there was much I could've done to avoid getting screwed. My invitation to the game wasn't really an invitation but an order, and I couldn't have refused to play even if I'd known in advance what I was in for. And for the rest of that school year I played in the jockstraps' poker game under the same sort of summons numerous times, though I made up beaucoup excuses not to play whenever I could. Thank God I won every time, because I suspect that if I'd lost, I would have had to pay in hard-earned cash or risk having my head shoved into the whirlpool down in the training room. As it was I collected many more IOUs that fall and spring, converted a pittance of what I won into cash as the months rolled by, and got pretty good at recognizing the jockstraps' signatures no matter how illegible they were. From my sophomore year on I lived off campus, so ducking the jockstrap action became a whole lot easier. The unclaimed IOUs went into the garbage over a quarter century ago.

So much for my first college poker game. If the extent of the on-campus action had been in the athletic dorm, I might've attended more classes and done more homework throughout college, and thus might've achieved my goal of being a lawyer or a Wall Street tycoon. But the jockstraps' game wasn't the only one in town, of course, and the following day's events, once and for all, short-circuited my career as an outstanding student all to hell.

The ole devil appeared to me just after breakfast my second day on campus, in the form of the calm-eyed guy who'd been the other winner in the jockstrap game the night before. This guy will be a continuing character, ducking in and out of my life for the duration of this book, and since the term "that calm-eyed guy" tends to grate on one after a hundred repetitions or so, let's give him a name. How 'bout Steve? Okay, Steve (and I haven't seen him in twenty years and don't even know if he's alive, and the last time I saw him he wanted to talk to me about Jesus) was in school on a football scholarship, but he wasn't your average jock. He'd been a highly recruited high school player who'd decided not to go to college; gotten married and made his living in back-street poker rooms for a couple of years, both as a dealer and a player; and finally accepted a scholarship only after his marriage had broken up. He was older than most other students and about a hundred times more streetwise. He was also movie-star handsome, with thick, dark hair and piercing blue eyes, and he had some of the most gorgeous beauties on campus panting nonstop after him. For the next couple of years, I was to emulate this guy in the same way that kids of that era tried to act like Steve McQueen. Fortunately for me, he was one helluva poker player; if he'd been a real sucker at the table, impressionable me likely would've copied his style of play and gone right down the tube.

But I'm getting a little bit ahead of myself. When Steve stopped me on campus on my second morning as a college student, I knew zero about the guy other than that I'd played in one poker game with him in which he'd folded a lot. I was hustling along between buildings, headed for the chow hall, when he seemed to materialize from behind a tree and called out, "Hold it, there, freshman."

I stopped in my tracks and stood at attention. I wondered if he was about to use his upperclassman status to strip me of the fifteen bucks I'd managed to collect out of the twenty with which I'd bought into the game in the athletic dorm.

He tried to keep a straight face but couldn't and broke up laughing. "Look," he said, "you can stand at ease and dispense with the 'sir' bullshit. That stuff's for the kids around here. If we can make the right deal, I'm gonna take you to a poker game."

I relaxed. "You mean *now*? It's not even eight o'clock in the morning."

"Right now," Steve said. "They've been playin' all night, and if you'll keep 'em close to the vest the same as you did in that game yesterday, you gotta win."

I thought about yesterday's game and didn't want any more IOUs. "Sorry, but I've got class," I said. "And besides, I didn't even get my buy-in back, and I can't buy a thing with all this paper I'm holding."

"This game's cash, and there's a helluva lot more of it where this cash comes from. You'll win. Trust me. You'll win."

The second the word *cash* popped out of his mouth, I knew I was about to depart from the straight-student path for the second day in a row. I needed money. I'd drained my bank account to pay for my tuition and books, and other than the dormitory deposit, I'd yet to come across with room and board. My job as football manager was to get me a 50 percent return on my tuition and books, but I didn't know that at the time. I could've depended on my parents for the rest, but any funds from my dad came with Sunday-go-to-meetin' strings attached. I said, "Where *is* this game?"

"First things first," Steve said. "Santa Claus I'm not, and I'm not letting any foxes in this henhouse unless I get something for it. Twenty-five percent of your winnings it'll cost you. That's my fee."

I was puzzled. "For today?"

"Forever," Steve said. "Every time you play in this here poker game, from now on."

I frowned. "Say, now. We're not gonna pass each other any cards, are we?"

"Man, I'm a lover, not a cheater. We don't pull one bit of funny business. You think I'd chance getting kicked out of the game? I don't cheat, and I'd damned sure better not catch you doin' it."

In my hand I carried a spiral notebook with a ballpoint pen clipped to the pages. I looked toward the dining hall, down at the notebook, and back at Steve. I said, "I guess I could play for a couple of hours."

Steve started to walk away at a pretty good clip, then stopped and looked back at me. "What're you waitin' on?" he said. "If we got a deal on the twenty-five percent, we're on our way."

And so much for my second day of class. Steve led the way on a three-block walk to the Phi Delt Fraternity House, and when he started up the steps to the red brick building with the four white pillars holding up the porch awning, I thought he must've led me on a wild goose chase, and suspected that I was in for some more upperclassman-versus-the-freshman bullshit where I'd have to do some goofy stunt at Steve's direction. But I wasn't in for anything like that, not at all. Steve took me through a lobby with padded carpet on the floor, and then up two flights of stairs, and in a few minutes we were in the attic. I was about to play in my second attic poker game in two days, but trying to compare the layout where the Phi Delts played with the jockstraps' quarters was like setting a brand new Beemer alongside a fifteen-year-old Chevy that's headed for the wrecking yard and asking a guy which one he'd rather drive.

The Phi Delt poker palace was finished out with hardwood flooring, dropped acoustical ceiling, and two different clusters of easy chairs arranged around small coffee tables, with individual floor lamps casting soft light on the tables and chairs. The tables and chairs sat on big, round designer throw rugs.

Dead center in the room a green-shaded lamp hung by a cord from the ceiling, and underneath the lamp sat the kind of elegant poker table that doesn't exist anymore—an octagon with eight divided spaces for players to set their chips, and with round drink holders in each of the spaces. The center of the table was covered in padded leather. There were five players in the game, fraternity boys cut from the same cookie-cutter mold, slim waisted with full heads of sandy brown hair, each guy wearing a knit shirt with an alligator on the breast pocket, the frat boy's uniform. Nike and Janzen and Hilfiger had yet to cast their spells on American campuses, and wouldn't for another couple of decades, so for the frat rats of the late 1950s the word was Izod, the symbol an alligator, and rushees either wore Izod or could forget about getting a bid.

I followed Steve over and stood looking at the action. Christ, the Phi Delts even had new cards, and not just one deck but six, two in play at all times, with four standbys unopened and still in the cellophane stacked off to one side. The decks in use were a red one and a blue one, and while one player dealt the red cards the next guy in line shuffled the blue deck, so that one deck was always ready to go as soon as a hand was over. The dealer had called for a seven-card stud game, and as the upcards followed the two down cards a joker appeared, wild with aces, straights, and flushes. The joker counted as an ace for high-card purposes so that the player with the exposed joker had first action. He tossed a couple of chips in the pot. I blinked.

Now these were poker chips, the absolute, positive real fucking thing, clay pieces stamped with a grid pattern and monogrammed with a G. Later I'd learn that one of the frat rats' dads had ordered the chips from the same place in Las Vegas that furnished the casinos, that there'd been a flaw in the monogram the first time around, and that the flawed chips had ended up with junior at the frat house. The only poker chips I'd ever seen were either cheap light plastic or cardboard, both of which you could buy at Walgreen's for about ten cents a gross. The chips at the Phi Delt House had cost—as one of the frat boys told me proudly one day—a quarter *apiece*. Christ, but those chips were gorgeous. In later years I've owned several even finer and more expensive sets, but I'll never forget my first glimpse at the real pro-player poker chips in the Phi Delt game.

Just like the jockstraps, the Phi Delts smoked, but they'd furnished expensive glass ashtrays to every player and there wasn't a Coke bottle in sight, as either an ash disposal or a spittoon. Those who were drinking had Styrofoam cups, and in the corner of the room sat an icemaker. The thick cloud of cigarette smoke that hovered over the jockstraps' game was missing here, and I looked up as a ceiling exhaust fan chugged away. I wondered if I'd died and gone to heaven. There I stood in the midst of splendor, wearing dirty sneakers, jeans with holes worn in the knees, and a plain white T-shirt. One of the poker players showed me a bored, distasteful look, then returned his attention to his hand.

Steve asked if there were seats open. One of the frat boys gestured at a vacant chair, then eyed me dubiously until Steve gave his verbal okay. The frat rat then nodded at me and pointed to the other empty seat. Steve pulled out forty dollars, four times his initial buy-in in the jockstrap game. I pulled out my wallet, extracted two tightly folded twenties from a secret compartment, and followed Steve's example. There was a fifty-cent limit in the jockstrap game, but the Phi Delts' limit was *two whole dollars*, about twice the stakes at any other game I'd ever played in.

The banker took our money and opened a cookie can. Inside the can were wads of twenties, and I spied one corner of a fifty-dollar bill. I'm sure my eyes bugged. After he closed the can, the banker pushed Steve and I equal stacks of chips, in half-dollar, dollar, and two-dollar denominations. We tossed in our antes and the next guy in line prepared to deal.

And away we went in Frat Boy Land.

As for the play itself, all in all the Phi Delts' game wasn't as Mad Hatter–like as the football players' game. Frat rat dealer's choices didn't include as many games featuring community cards in crisscross or zigzag patterns, and, thank God, no one dealt the "Eat Your Wallet" game, but there was a goes-on-forever stud game called Push Tiddle (it'd take several pages to describe Push Tiddle in detail, but, suffice it to say, each player had a choice between taking the card offered or sweetening the pot and accepting the next card off the deck), and jacks-or-better-to-open draw, though the Phi Delts didn't require trips to win, as had my high school buddies. The Phi Delts did play a lot of seven-card stud, hi-lo split, which over the next few years was to become my bread-and-butter game because of the way it favored the tightass. I learned very quickly to fold my hand in seven split unless I had three cards lower than six with no pairs on the deal and (not even Steve played the game as conservatively as I did, at least not until he thought it over and then decided to copy me) I also tossed away any three cards that would lead to a high hand. Here's why: I risked my money on college boy hi-lo split *only* when I could win both ways if I made a small straight or flush, and when I was a heavy favorite with my low hand if the flush or straight didn't materialize. Anyone playing a strictly high hand has only one way to win, and if the high hand fails to take half the pot, the player has no chance at low. Even when trips came on the deal, unless the player made a full house when all the cards were out, he would often lose. While three of a kind nearly always wins in high-only seven stud, hi-lo split is an entirely different proposition when low players often back into straights and flushes that they weren't really looking for. In hi-lo split as played among the college set, high-hand players lost out in the long run, period.

(The foregoing isn't true, by the way, in seven-card hi-lo played in casinos, nor in the game called Hi-Lo Omaha, a variation of Hold 'Em where each player gets four pocket cards instead of two, because in those two games, unless someone makes an eight low or better—called a qualifying hand—the holder of the high hand takes the entire pot. One of the World Series of Poker tournaments is high-only Omaha, an entirely different animal than hi-lo split and a game requiring a certain amount of skill, but Omaha played hi-lo reminds me of five-card blind racehorse, where no one ever looks at his or her hand until the bets are all in. Occasionally as you march through Poker Land you'll encounter Omaha games, and my advice would be to steer clear of 'em. Omaha is confusing to Hold 'Em players, because in Omaha you must use two pocket cards to go with three communities, and there are no hands made up of one in the pocket and four on the board. Personally I rate Omaha Hi-Lo's skill level right along with Eat Your Wallet's and Low Hole, High Spade's, and I believe that the so-called Omaha experts are in reality terribly weak Hold 'Em players who stand a chance to win only in Mickey Mouse games. The few times I've been forced to play Omaha Hi-Lo—in games where the person on the button has a choice between calling Hold 'Em or Omaha—I always folded unless I was dealt four high pocket cards two of which formed a pair. I probably haven't come out ahead over the years in Omaha Hi-Lo—and I seriously doubt that anyone else has, either, except for the house man, who's taking a rake out of the pot—but I really haven't played it often enough to develop a pattern history.)

We're talking about college poker here, however, where there's no qualifying requirement for a low hand, and the strategy that I used to beat college boy hi-lo games was dead-on. And as for the Phi Delt game, since it didn't have the unforgettable wrinkles that I'd experienced in the football players' game—the guys trying to keep their lights, the guys who split their chips in half, the IOUs and whatnot—time has dimmed my memory as to whether I won or lost the first time that Steve took me there, but over the next four years the Phi Delts were to furnish most of my drinking and partying money. There is one thing about the frat boy action that I'll never forget, and that is the fact that about half the Phi Delts, in addition to being rich kids, were much better poker players than I ever encountered in the jockstrap game. At least they were better than average *college* poker players, which wouldn't have made them a threat at the Golden Nugget and points west, but the game was alive with tightasses who played about the same way as I did. The remaining frat boys were bad enough players to make up for the skill of the better-than-average guys, however, and since the game was cash on the barrelhead, I could do much better at the Phi Delt house than in the attic at the athletic dorm even if I only won about half as much. And not only that, the Phi Delts played two-dollar limit—about four times the stakes in the jockstrap game—so all in all the profits available on Fraternity Row made any money made in the athletic dorm insignificant. Throughout the rest of my college days, on the occasions when I was able to duck the jockstraps—probably a couple times a week, when the sore-assed running back or Raw Meat failed to collar me and issue me a summons before I could hustle out of the training room after practice—I made a lot of hay along Fraternity Row and, due to the size of my bankroll rather than the rakish good looks I envisioned myself having in those days, dated some of the best-looking girls in school. I'll never know if a case of the shorts would have left me dateless, but, thank God, I never had to find out.

And I think I should mention here that even though I came to really like the jockstrap crowd, and count a lot of has-been football players among my closest friends even today, I had the typical poor boy's resentment of the rich fraternity guys. Their conversations bored me to death, and I hated every minute of their company during their frat house poker games. My spirit soared only when it came to cash-in time.

And with the foregoing statements, dear readers, here comes the poker lesson to be learned from my experience in the football players' game versus my experience in the Phi Delts' game, in the form of another Poker Pigeon's Postulate: **No matter how soft or how rugged the competition, playing poker with** people who have no money to lose is a total waste of time. This is true in games where a tightass is practically assured that he'll win, as *I* was in the jockstrap game, and is doubly true in modern Texas Hold 'Em, where the biggest suckers imaginable occasionally beat the best players in the world. The number one mistake *I* see among really good players is that they continue to play daily in the toughest games in town that also feature the smallest bankrolls merely because they like the other players personally, when their time would be much better spent looking for a softer spot to land.

At first glance it seems as if I've once again stated the obvious, but that's not true in this case. There aren't that many ways to know your opponents' strengths and weaknesses as players until you've played with them a number of times, but it's pretty easy to figure out whether or not there is ample cash in the game the very first time you sit down. Watch for players making short buys and going all in in limit games, and keep your eyes and ears open to learn whether players in the game are borrowing from each other. Players' demeanor when suffering bad beats is another dead giveaway; well-heeled folks are disappointed but philosophical when the cards break against them, whereas the broke's reaction to a bad beat is total panic. Although it's true that where casino card rooms are legal you will have no worry about collecting your winnings when you come out on top, *the mere fact that the game goes on in a casino with a cash-in, chips-out policy is no guarantee that there is sufficient cash in the game to make it worth your while to play.* There are certain expenses involved in traveling to any casino (unless you live in the same town as the casino, and that's not likely, because only those living in certain cities can find a game just down the street, and in nearly every other part of the country the casinos are either out in the sticks on an Indian reservation or in a boat docked someplace along the Mississippi), so not only must you win, but you must also cover gas, meals, and hotel rooms, and there are many poker games where covering your expenses and making a profit simply isn't possible. Let me share an experience that I had in the so-called gambling Mecca of the world.

Other than World Series of Poker time, when the action is plentiful at all limits and levels, I hadn't been to Las Vegas in over twenty years until this past spring. My pride and joy are my kids, who have made business successes while their old man sits around trying to catch two aces, and earlier this year my eldest had business in Las Vegas that required him to be in town for about a week. He offered me hard-earned Advantage miles to pay for my ticket to meet him out west, and I was tickled to death to go. My son had had his formal education and was now ready for some lessons at the table. And, boy, was I ever going to show him a few!

You may think that you can see this one coming from a mile away, but my Las Vegas experience worked out differently than you'd expect. I stayed downtown at the Golden Nugget, because in the Las Vegas I knew and remembered, the Golden Nugget was the spot to play a little poker. My son and daughter-in-law were at the Venetian, which other than some pretty amazing special effects—I'm talking about the area where you think you're outside and really you're still in the building, and the ceiling is done in clouds and stars and whatnot—and some awesome food at Wolfgang Puck's, just isn't my kind of place. But, dammit, neither is the Golden Nugget any longer.

My son sat behind me as an observer as I saddled up to a game at the Nugget, a game where I really caught some cards, and where the tourists playing were about the worst at Hold 'Em that I'd ever seen. The long and short of it is, I was the big winner by miles, and as the tourists came and went I sat there for hours picking their pockets. My son was impressed. When I was ready to cash in, it took six racks to hold my chips.

My kid walked proudly behind me as I shoved the racks across the counter, then watched the teller pop new bills into a stack and hand them over. As we left the window, I thumbed through the money and counted it. I'd won a shade over four hundred dollars.

My son's face fell a bit, though he tried hard not so show his disappointment. Christ, I think he makes more than four hundred bucks every single day of the year.

The game that I'd just blitzed was three and six-dollar limit, and the four hundred dollars I'd won was about the maximum possible at that level. Had I been in town on a serious money-making mission, as I usually am, my winnings would have barely covered my hotel bill. Back in the 1970s, we played ten and twenty and twenty and forty every day at the Nugget, and after many a trip I went home with a four- or five-thousand-dollar profit, but that was when Steve Winn owned the hotel and Bill Boyd ran the poker room. An entirely different world than the one we live in today, in other words. I checked at several other downtown poker parlors. Three and six was the biggest game within five or six blocks of the intersection of Fremont and Las Vegas Boulevard.

So I violated my own postulate and decided to play in a game where what I could win wouldn't be worth the time that I'd spend at the table. I knew where the only modern-day big games in town were located, though I had misgivings about playing there. I loaded my kid into a cab, and we steamed out on the Strip to the Bellagio. The Bellagio sports one of the world's biggest-action poker rooms. I knew that, and I also knew some of the players at the Bellagio from the old days, and I also understood that the Bellagio was one of the toughest places in the country to play for anyone wanting to make a living at the game. But, what the hell, I wanted to impress my kid.

The Bellagio's poker room is in two sections, with a step-up platform leading into the high-rollers' lair, an area separated from the cheaper games by white wooden railings and trellises. "Cheap" games start at eight- and sixteen-dollar limit in the front part near the entry and graduate upward as you near the step-up, with everything past the step-up thirty and sixty and above. Just how high the games get in the enclosure depends on who's around on that particular day, with limits going to four thousand and eight thousand if certain high-dollar pros are in action. I saw a few familiar faces in the big-time games, nodded to a few guys, but stayed downstairs and fell into a fifteen-and-thirty game. My son dragged up a chair and sat behind me.

And of course I'd saddled up to as tough a poker game as there is, a game where everyone plays dead on, one of the only games I've played in where I didn't feel as if I was a favorite to win (nor was I a great underdog either, but once the skill of play reaches a certain level, who wins and who loses hinges on who happens to catch the cards that day). I played four or five hours and lost a couple hundred bucks, and around dusk I cashed in my chips and left the poker room.

None of the foregoing makes for a life-changing incident, and so far, at any rate, my son hasn't disowned me, but my experience out west is a good example of the advice I'm giving here. If you're going to play poker for profit, you simply must find games where (1) you can win enough money to make the game worth your while, and (2) the play isn't so skillful that you have no advantage. There are games in Las Vegas that I can beat like a drum, but those games are too small to cover expenses, and the Las Vegas games where the stakes are high enough to make them worthwhile are populated with the best players in the world. So give me the casino games in Oklahoma, Louisiana, and Mississippi, and you can have Las Vegas and welcome to it. I've seen enough of the Strip at this point to last me until I die.

5

I Meet Hold 'Em

or,
The Intricate Nuances of Playing Jack-Five

Having the old boxer primed and ready to jump the hijackers didn't help my nerves, but when Monkey One and Monkey Two began to bring the players, one at a time, into the bedroom with their hands zip cuffed behind them, strip them of their bankrolls, and then leave them lying on the floor while they went to lie in wait for the next player to arrive, I managed to relax just a little. By the time there were seven or eight of us tied up, I was pretty sure that they wouldn't shoot us as long as we cooperated. All I had to do was keep the boxer under control.

And just as I was breathing a bit easier, Monkey One brought another player into the room, sat him down, and turned to leave. As Monkey One neared the hallway, the boxer whispered in my ear, "I got one hand loose. Next time that sonofabitch comes in here, you fall off the bed. He'll come over to check on you, and that's when I'll lower the boom on the guy."

You've probably had enough of college boy poker, and we're just about to move on. But before we do, hey, *time out*. We'll get along to pro-style poker shortly, but this is the ideal spot to insert a most important poker lesson. I'll begin with an anecdote and then go from there.

A number of years after my introduction to college-style poker, I was seated in a game—one with a slightly more professional atmosphere—alongside Cowboy Wolford. In case you haven't heard of Cowboy, you should have, and if you'd like to see his picture, take a stroll through Binnion's and check out the Poker Hall of Fame.

This game was backroom, peer-in-through-a-slot-in-the-door-and-whisper-that-Joe-sent-you illegal, held in a condemned building on a dusty old street deep in the heart of Texas, with an exhaust fan *chug-chugging* in the background and a guy who looked sort of like Frankenstein's Igor guarding the door. Around midafternoon on this particular day, Igor stumped up to the poker table and announced that someone he didn't recognize was at the door asking to get in the game. There were two questions that needed answering before admitting someone to one of those speakeasy poker joints back in those days: (1) Is the guy a cop? and (2) Did he bring cash with him? Igor had scribbled the newcomer's name on a scrap of paper and now passed the slip over to Cowboy.

Cowboy squinted to decipher Igor's handwriting. Finally, Cowboy's lips spread slowly into a smile. He nodded and passed the paper down the table. He said to Igor, "Let the boy in."

The paper made the length of the table, going from hand to hand, and finally came to rest in front of Bob Hooks (another Poker Hall of Famer, or if he isn't in the Hall, he oughtta be). Hooks, a big hulk of a former college football player, silently read the name, his lips moving as he did, then shot Cowboy a worried glance and shook his head. Obviously Hooks didn't know the newcomer at the door.

"I'm vouchin' for the boy," Cowboy said. "I met him at a game in California. Paid his way through college playin' poker."

This one broke Hooks up. "One-ah them, huh?" He looked at the ceiling, rolled his eyes, and let out a belly laugh.

I was fairly new to the game back then, so I was totally confused. I said to Cowboy, "What the hell is so funny?" I was a by-God college man myself and didn't appreciate these guys snickering at my brothers in the cap and gown.

Cowboy looked me over. He grinned. "Son," he finally said, "you've been around here a while, so now I can tell you. The only reason we ever let you in this here game to begin with was that you said you played a lot of poker in college. Truth be told, son, we just love these fuckin' college guys."

And truth be told, dear reader, some forty years later I can state with authority that real professional poker players do, indeed, "love these fuckin' college guys." What follow are The Poker Pigeon's College Guy Postulates explaining why:

1. **Almost no one who claims to have paid his or her way through college playing poker really did so. Real poker sharks don't advertise, and for anyone who is new to a game, yet brags about having paid his or her way through college, trade school, night school, or any other school, for that matter, by playing poker, if they were telling the truth, it would be akin to a bank robber strolling into a police station and announcing which bank he or she plans to rob and what time the heist is coming off. It's been my experience that anyone claiming to be a poker shark is 99 percent certain to be easy money once he or she gets into a game. With few exceptions, college students rely on (1) student loans or (2) the sweat from Mommy and Daddy's brow to get by. Since student loan funds flow**

directly to the college to pay the student's bill without ever crossing the student's hot little palm, and since Mommy and Daddy are nearly always flat broke after paying for college and have no money to furnish junior's gambling habit, the idea that anyone has fleeced his or her fellow students for enough to pay his or her tuition and room and board is, in nearly all cases, preposterous. I won a lot of money in college—at least it seemed a lot at the time—but like most novice gamblers, *I* spent my winnings on booze and women, so I still had to work sixty-hour weeks during the summer and act as a servant to a bunch of pampered jockstraps during the school year to make it.

2. In the rare instances where the claimee actually did win all or a portion of his or her college expenses, then having that recent graduate in the game is *even better* for the pro than having the compulsive bullshitter who didn't actually win any of his college tuition at the poker table. Anyone who actually won a lot of money in college is likely to have a pretty good bankroll. But since he or she is accustomed to playing in college poker games, where the level of competition he or she has faced hasn't been high, this person will be the ultimate sucker and will require several years to adjust his or her thinking to the point that he or she can be a winner in the real poker world. This statement will rankle those youngsters who have found success at the World Series of Poker in recent years, but all of these collegeboy final table appearances—after the students have won their seats in Internet tournaments with buy-in fees of as little as five bucks—only bolster my belief that in a freeze-out tournament where the blinds increase dramatically as the participants near

the finish line, anyone can win and the pro is no more of a favorite in the main event than the guy who rode in on a turnip truck. The proof is found in these Boy Wonders' fates *after* their big wins at the WSOP. All college boys with newfound humongous bankrolls will be invited to play in private cash games with Las Vegas pros, and those foolish enough to accept the invitations—and just about 100 percent of the "up and coming youngsters" believe themselves invincible and are dying to play against the world-famous pros—will be lucky to emerge with their underwear intact. the real tragedy is that so many of the college kids who come out a winner at the WSOP drop out of college expecting an easy life as a poker professional, but within a short period of time they lose their bankrolls, and at that point their lack of money pretty well ends their chances of returning to school and getting their degree. Success in one big poker tournament is no more of an indicator of future success as a professional than someone hitting a slot machine jackpot is an indicator that the person will beat the slots from now on. No one should consider quitting school or his or her day job without several years of profitable experience under his or her belt. Over the years I have known many times more people who have ruined their lives playing poker than have been successful at it. A bit soapboxy on my part, maybe, but that's the way it is. I've got a heart and *I* feel for these people, and that might be another reason that *I* no longer play at the level that I used to.

Do I ever wish that someone had given me this advice at the end of my first college year, though I probably wouldn't have listened any more than today's youngsters. I'd won a lot of money during the spring semester, and within just a few months my old buddy Steve would introduce me to some poker games where I had no business playing. Steve had insisted on getting 25 percent of my winnings before he'd introduce me to the college soft spot, but for some reason he didn't ask for a percentage when he introduced me to the pros. Whether or not the gang of pros had to kick back to Steve in order to get him to bring me around, I've never known, but truthfully, I wouldn't be surprised if they had had to. Steve was pretty much a dyed-in-the-wool mercenary, a sell-you-out-before-you-sell-me-out kind of guy.

Which, by the way, is pretty much the attitude one must have to make it in the poker world. Big lesson coming up, readers. This chapter is where I'll describe my adjustment from other forms of poker to Hold 'Em and outline how, through often painful trial and error, I came to understand what it takes to be a success playing two out of your hand with five on the board.

By the end of my freshman year I had pocketfuls of hangin' around cash, but I'd also accumulated a big list of cut classes, late term papers, etc., etc., etc. I missed flunking out by the skin of my teeth and received a letter from the dean placing me on probation for the following year. Even after I read the letter I wasn't worried; I didn't believe that there was a course I couldn't pass, though I think it ticked me off that school was about to interfere with my poker playing.

My buddy Steve fared even worse than I, academically, but that was only because he'd had one more year to screw up than I had had, and at the end of his sophomore year he got his walking papers. No more football scholarship, no more school. Steve couldn't have cared less. He rented an apartment a few blocks from the campus, built himself an oblong poker table, complete with sponge rubber cover and seating for ten, and started running a game.

One day about the middle of summer, I stood on the back lot of a Firestone store changing a truck tire. The temperature was about a hundred. I remember that the tire was one of the really dangerous types, one that you had to put inside a steel cage before you aired it up, because the entire rim could come blasting out of the center of the tire at about 150 miles an hour and kill someone. I was rolling the tire into the cage when someone called my name. I mopped sweat from my forehead and turned to find Steve standing there.

And not just Steve. Beside him was a curvy blonde wearing tight shorts and a halter top. Her arm was loosely about his waist. He wore khakis and a golf shirt, and sunglasses, and he was sipping a Coke. He said, "Are you having fun?"

I didn't see any point in answering, and I think I just looked at him.

He swigged Coke. There was frost on the bottle. "I'm running a game I'm cutting down for a hundred bucks a night. Twenty-five percent is yours, if you want to help me."

My throat was burning. "What do I gotta do?"

"Keep up with the take, mainly. Game's dealer's choice, so you won't have to deal any. Play a little if you want, but the limit's pretty high. Three- and five-dollar limit."

The two-dollar game at the Phi Delt house was the biggest game I'd seen thus far.

"Mostly," Steve said, "you'd have to spell me some, take over so I can get away. The game goes on all night sometimes. You'd have to stay with it as long as there're players. Probably means you'll have to move in with me. I got an extra bedroom. Got a courtyard with a pool. You living at the dormitory?"

"For now," I said.

"They got a curfew. You'd have to get outta there and bring your stuff over to my place."

I considered my options for about thirty seconds. Help Steve run a poker game, or change truck tires in hundred-degree heat for seventy-five cents an hour. "When do you want me to start?" I said.

"Game starts at six o'clock," Steve said. "You'd have to take a shower and clean up, so better get a move on."

"Just like that? I might have to give notice."

"Aw, they can get all kinds of guys to do what you're doing, changing tires," Steve said. "Course, I can't make you." He squeezed the blonde. "This is Toni," Steve said. "She serves the drinks in the game."

I think I was halfway to the office to turn in my resignation before the words were out of his mouth.

And so began my first venture outside the law, though I was too wet behind the ears to know that what we were doing was illegal. In later years I played in many games with steel doors and people with shotguns guarding the entry from invasion, but the game at Steve's apartment was populated with college guys he'd lured away from their studies or summer jobs, and it looked more like a bunch of "the guys" getting together on Wednesday to drink beer and play a little penny ante. The stakes were more than I'd ever seen; it was pretty easy to win *a hundred bucks* playing three and five, so for the first couple of weeks I didn't play. I was plenty busy because—and even then I wasn't so naïve that I wasn't prepared for this—Steve expected me to do about 100 percent of the game running in return for my 25 percent of the take, the result being that he played as much as he wanted while I collected the take. The take was three dollars an hour per player and the game stayed full—seven handed—about twenty hours a day, and it was nothing unusual for the rake to equal four hundred a day, about twice what the luckiest player in the house could expect to win. Within a couple of weeks I had a roll of hundred-dollar bills in my pocket, so I began to sit in as a player whenever I could.

Which wasn't very often, because of Steve's insistence that the playing time allotted to him didn't apply to me. It wasn't long before Steve was actually a full-time player and I was running the game—though he kept his eye on the till and made sure to collect his 75 percent—and I'm fairly certain that if the law had busted us it would've been me toted off to jail while Steve stood around squeezing Toni.

And speaking of her: Toni was a bit more than just the drink waitress. She did hustle beer and soft drinks for tips when the mood struck her, but what she mostly did was lie around on Steve's bed reading romance novels. Occasionally Steve would go in with her, close the door, and not emerge for several hours. The door to the bedroom was right beside the kitchen entry, and I can't tell you how many times I trudged past on my way to fix Cokes and beer for the players with Toni's moans and heavy breathing ringing in my ears.

Not that I'm complaining. Steve had opened the door to a new world, one that I wasn't to leave for a couple of decades, and I really liked what I was seeing of it. My pockets were always full, a situation that has never occurred during the few times in my life that I've held a job, and even though I didn't average over four hours of sleep every twenty-four, I was plenty young and don't recall feeling tired. The "life" had me pumped, I suppose, my adrenaline racing through my body like caffeine.

(I think this is a good time to insert a word about running poker games in general. Several times during my poker life I've turned to running games in order to build a bankroll, though I never stuck with running the game for longer than required to build my cash reserve. Most of the games I had anything to do with running happened in the years when Nevada was the only state where all forms of gambling were legal, though New Jersey voted in gambling—restricted to Atlantic City—a few years before I resigned as a pro and reached my current pigeon sta-

tus. America operates on a strange moral compass; people will flock
in droves to states where gambling is legal, yet they will denounce
the gamblers who make their livings under the radar in their hometowns as petty criminals. While poker game runners generally make
a lot more money than any professional player, successfully running a poker game is not a lazy man's profession, and it also involves risk that I believe far exceeds the reward. You must stay
with the game round the clock, sometimes going without sleep
for days on end, and you must keep a closer lookout for cheaters
than you do when you are playing on your own money, because
a gang of cheats can run off your legitimate players in a hurry.
You must also risk losing a lot of money to employee thieves
[mostly dealers] and people who gamble on credit—it's impossible to avoid running tabs on occasion—and on the worst end
of the scale, going to jail, or, as we'll see as my life story rolls
on, falling victim to hijackers who may or may not shoot you.
So while running a game isn't something I'd recommend to most
folks, it beats dodging creditors all to hell.)

As I said before, Steve had married out of high school and
had spent two years playing and dealing in illegal poker rooms
before accepting his football scholarship. In the on-campus games
in which I'd played with him he'd pretty much gone along with
the games that the other guys wanted to play, but now that he
was the game runner, he began to dig up some poker games
when it was his deal that none of the rest of us had heard of.
One of these games was called Shotgun Low. It was actually five-
card lowball draw with two extra bets: the betting opened when
each player had three cards, then continued after the fourth card
dealt, after the fifth card dealt, and then after the draw. At least
that's the way Steve explained it to us mopes, though the game
is as different from five-card draw as Hold 'Em is from seven-
card stud. I don't want to wade off into Shotgun Low strategy
(which could be another book in itself), but suffice it to say that

it's a dealer-controlled game, that Steve was light-years ahead of everyone else in lowball savvy, and that he beat that poker game almost to death by calling Shotgun Low nearly every time it was his turn to deal.

(If you're not familiar with the term, dealer-controlled games are forms of poker where the dealer—or the player on the button in casino play—has a tremendous leg up on all other players because of his or her position. Hold 'Em is a prime example of such a game, though there are others. Where the dealer has last action during each and every betting round, he or she gets to see what all the other players are going to do before he or she has to act, and that's such an advantage that you'll see very good players coming into pots with incredibly weak starting hands if they have the button. Shotgun Low is even more of a dealer-advantaged game than Hold 'Em, and the only reason that you never see Shotgun Low in casinos is that no more than seven can play because of the number of cards coming off the deck during the deal. Since the high hand showing acts first during each betting round in five- and seven-card stud, pros usually steer clear of those games, because there is no dealer advantage.)

On the few occasions that Steve didn't deal Shotgun Low in the game at his apartment, he introduced us to another game that he'd learned in the back-alley poker parlors. The game was called Hold 'Em.

Have I mentioned that Steve learned his poker in his home state of New Mexico? The game commonly referred to as Texas Hold 'Em probably didn't originate in Texas at all; it's true that Texas boys carried Hold 'Em to Las Vegas with them, but before that, someone imported Hold 'Em to Texas. I played regularly in a game a few decades back where the door guard was a usually drunk older guy who had once worked for the Seven-Up bottling company, and who had kept his old uniforms and answered the poker parlor door with a soft drink emblem sewn on his shirt pocket. We called him Seven-Up Red. He was from Colorado, and one late evening he told us that he'd played Hold 'Em in Denver in the 1920s, but that back then the game was known as Love and Affection. I swear he said that, though you should take Red's love for liquor into consideration when evaluating the story, and if Hold 'Em were called Love and Affection today, it's doubtful that it would be near as popular. Regardless, even though Texas Hold 'Em is the most commonly heard name of the game, the game almost certainly didn't originate in Texas.

Steve only dealt Hold 'Em a few times and gave up very quickly trying to turn the game into a Hold 'Em fest for a couple of very good reasons. First of all, it's damned near impossible to interest a bunch of stud and draw poker players in Hold 'Em, especially if they've never played Hold 'Em before, because the game is at first so foreign to anything they've ever seen. When confronted with Hold 'Em, even players who came into virtually every pot in stud or draw would quickly toss their cards away. Players get hooked on Hold 'Em by playing in games where Hold 'Em is the only game permitted, and once they get over the confusion of seeing people raising multiple times with only two cards in their hands and none on the board, Hold 'Em quickly becomes the only game that they're interested in playing. It's addictive.

The other reason that Steve gave up on introducing Hold 'Em on a regular basis had to do with the ante structure. In our game only the dealer anted, though he could add an ante for the other players by putting up an equal amount in addition to his original ante. Hold 'Em is played with at least one, usually two, and sometimes three or more blinds (forced bets), with the largest blind equaling the smaller of the two betting limits, and without the forced bets becomes pretty pointless. You'd have to try playing Hold 'Em with no forced bets in order to appreciate what a crappy poker game it turns into, but take my word for it that without the forced-bet feature, Hold 'Em never would have been heard of.

So while I did learn the rules of Hold 'Em during the few times that Steve introduced it, I knew nothing about the game other than the rules and had no interest in learning more. That situation, however, was just about to change.

You remember summers, don't you, back when you were in school, three whole months that wore endlessly on and on? By the end of July that year I had more money than I'd ever dreamed of having—over a thousand bucks, as I recall. School was scheduled to start in about six weeks, and for some reason I still considered myself a college student. I'd been up all night every night running the poker game while Steve slept in, screwed Toni's brains out, and played a little poker when the mood struck him. I decided to take the rest of the summer off. One morning after I'd cleaned up the poker game mess, I went in and told Steve what I was going to do.

I'm not sure what I expected him to say. The guy was my hero. I was really relieved when he acted as if he thought my idea was a great one. Said he needed time to relax, just as I did. Whatever I'd profited from the poker game take, Steve had made three times as much, not to mention that he'd played in the game twenty or thirty times and had never booked a loser. Also not to mention that without poker, he still had Toni to occupy his time.

So we shut down the game with no fanfare, and doing so was a lot easier than I expected. Around midafternoon the phone calls started to come in from the players, and as I told each and every one that our game was no more, they all seemed to accept the news stoically. In fact, I really didn't have to field many calls at all, because after I'd given the news to two or three guys, the word spread fast. As the game's normal time approached, there wasn't a single knock on the door. There's a lesson to be learned from this. In later years I've run games for varying periods of time, all the way from a month up to an entire year, but I've always made it a point to close down before the game became too well known. The guys I've known who were busted for illegal poker games kept the game going in the same place for much longer than was reasonable. Nathan Detroit's crap game didn't float just to be floating, and poker game runners should follow Nathan's example.

So anyway, *abra cadabra*, end of the poker game at Steve's apartment. No more staying up all night and no more food and drinks to serve. I went to bed around seven o'clock, slept for fourteen hours, and woke up feeling better than I had in months. I put on my swim trunks and went out by the pool, got involved in a water volleyball game, and met a few girls who'd been living around me all summer, but whom, due to being up to my ankles in the poker game every night, I'd never seen before. I was like the groundhog on Groundhog Day, only seeing my shadow didn't send me scurrying for cover.

And by five o'clock in the afternoon I was so bored that I couldn't sit still.

I hoisted myself out of the pool and trudged back to the apartment, dripping water every step; took a shower and toweled myself dry; then puzzled over exactly what was wrong. I had the weight of running the poker game off my shoulders and clear sailing ahead for the rest of the summer. As I dressed in my room I was jittery, completely on edge, a feeling I hadn't experienced before.

For the readers who haven't yet figured it out, I suffered from the same malady that strikes all poker players from time to time: the need to play poker. It's a hard sensation to describe, the slight tremors in the hands and arms, the numbness in the feet. One day in the distant future this same feeling would come over me and greatly influence my decision to fade off into the background forever, but at the moment, I was nineteen years old and invincible, and certain that whatever was wrong would go away on its own.

Once I was dressed I went into the other bedroom to check on Steve. He stood in front of the mirror combing his hair, the old fifties trick where he smoothed his hair back with his left hand as he combed with his right. He laid down the comb and watched me in the mirror.

"Maybe I shouldn't have called off the poker game," I said.

He looked amused. "It was your idea. You been working hard, and I wasn't gonna stop you."

I stuffed my hands into my pockets. "But now I got the itch to play."

He turned around and leaned a hip against the dresser. "You're a poker player. There'd be something wrong if you didn't want to play. I'm going to a game tonight, if you want to tag along."

"What game?"

"A guy I know from the joints back home. He's running a game here. It's all Hold 'Em."

"That two-card shit?"

Steve brushed lint from his sleeve. "That two-card shit. Right. But I'll tell you something. It's a game you'd better learn."

And so began my first-ever visit to a real-live underground poker parlor. The game itself was on the second floor of a rickety old building in the easternmost part of town, and we reached it from the street by climbing stairs that creaked and groaned under our feet. Steve pounded on the door. An eye appeared, magnified through a peephole. Chains rattled and the door swung wide. A man in his undershirt stood aside to let us pass, propping a double-barreled shotgun against the wall as he did.

Inside, under single bulbs suspended from the ceiling, sat two round poker tables, their cloth tops stretched tightly over hard foam rubber. The men playing were in their forties and older; I was the youngest person in the room—except for Steve—by a couple of decades. Only one of the tables was in use; Steve introduced me to the game runner, a short bald man named Mel, and Mel invited us to sit in. The game was five and ten, a healthy bump up from the highest limits I'd ever played before, and I'd never played Texas Hold 'Em at all other than in the few hands that Steve had dealt in the apartment game. There were two seats open. Steve took one and I took the other. I followed Steve's lead and bought in for two hundred dollars.

I was about as nervous as I had ever been, or have been since. My first poker games had been with guys I'd grown up with. Later on in college I'd played in games where I was clearly the best player. Neither situation existed here; I was surrounded by older men who looked very much in the know, and the size of the stakes made me taste dust in my mouth. In later years I've played much, much higher, of course, but my feeling the first time I played no-limit with hundreds of thousands of dollars at stake couldn't match my nervousness in that cramped upstairs room with an exhaust fan chugging away as I played five and ten.

Minutes later I was involved in my first-ever hand of Texas Hold 'Em, and I can remember my two pocket cards as if it were yesterday. I held the jack of hearts and the five of diamonds. And why does that one lousy hand so many years ago stick out in my mind? Because I won the pot, that's why.

And if you've been dozing through the most recent portion of this book, you'd better take notice here. I'm leading up to my own education as a poker player, and the thought processes that brought me from being a pure novice up to expert level. The transformation took several years, but every process must have its beginning. You've read that in my earliest days playing poker I learned to survive by being a tightass, and you've also heard me harp on my belief that a tightass simply cannot win in Hold 'Em.

So back to me at age nineteen, shiny tightass badge pinned to my chest, holding an offsuited jack-five in my first-ever Hold 'Em hand. The only thing I knew about the game was that I was to combine my two pocket cards with five cards dealt faceup in the center of the table to form the best possible poker hand that I could. I knew nothing of the odds of making this hand or that, or what two-card hand is favored over what other two-card hand, and my mind wasn't cluttered with position play or any of that other crap. I still wanted to play in tightass mode, but I had no idea what two cards in Texas Hold 'Em a tightass would play. I think I could have figured out that AA or KK was a pretty fair country hand even in that embryonic stage of my Hold 'Em development, but as far as any other two-card combination went, I hadn't a clue.

I wasn't in either blind position (the blinds in five and ten were two and five dollars), so I had nothing at risk when I picked up my jack-five. I could've tossed in my hand and not risked another penny on my jack-five, and while I wanted to continue my tightass ways, for all I knew, jack-five was a primo hand. I remember quite well that one player raised before it was my turn to act, so it was going to cost me fifteen dollars merely to see the first three cards that came out on the board.

I did know that if I *never* came into a pot I might as well not play in the game at all, so I altered my tightass strategy so that I wouldn't make any decisions as to whether or not to play in a pot until I'd seen the flop. My reasoning was that until I saw the first three cards on the board, I didn't know whether I had a hand or not. I was far off the mark, of course, but my novice reasoning wasn't nearly as bad as some of the strategies I've seen from players who've played Hold 'Em for years.

In my very first-ever Hold 'Em pot, the flop came 5,5,3.

Christ, I thought, *what an easy fucking game.*

I don't remember the size of the pot that I won. I do remember a couple of the players in the game, since they were to become regulars in games where I played for years, and I also recall that when I showed down my jack-five with a flourish, a couple of guys eyed me as if I were a large slab of rare prime rib. Since I'd won my very first pot I couldn't imagine that I'd done anything wrong, and I was about to embark on a month-long period of using my see-the-flop strategy to win several thousand dollars. I'd never dreamed there was that much money in the world.

In fact, if it hadn't have been for my first month as a Hold 'Em player, my book *Play Poker Like a Pigeon (and Take the Money Home)* never would have existed, the book you're reading now never would have been written, and I would have continued blithely on in the belief that there is only one correct way to play limit Hold 'Em—though no-limit is, has been, and always will be an entirely different game, and we'll get to that later on. I was definitely playing poker like a pigeon, but I was winning. What follows is (sort of) a defense of the strategy I used as a nineteen-year-old novice limit Hold 'Em player, and I believe to this day that, under the circumstances, my strategy wasn't nearly as bad as it sounds. Of course, it didn't hurt that the cards absolutely ran over me for that month, but like all poker players on a roll, I attributed my winnings to cagey play.

After I'd decided that I was going to see every flop, I stuck to my guns even though at times it would cost me two or three raises, in addition to the force, to do so, and I'm sure that the few giant pots that I won in that manner left many a poker player talking in his sleep. Once the flop appeared, however, my style of play changed dramatically. Today's players—even some of the so-called poker wizards—believe that once you've paid through the nose to look at the flop you are pot committed (whatever that is), and that if you catch the merest piece of what's on the board—or if the flop misses you entirely but you have two overcards (two pocket cards that are larger than any card on the board)—then you're supposed to see the pot through to the bitter end no matter the tariff, in the faint hope that you'll draw out on someone. I personally consider that strategy to be incredibly dumb no matter who is using it, and that the disciples of such nonsense lose many times more in such pots than they ever win on the few occasions when they catch the case cards that they are praying for in order to win.

Once the flop appeared, my strategy as a nineteen-year-old novice reverted to hard-line tightass mode; if I failed to flop a really strong hand I tossed my cards in at the hint of a bet from anyone at the table. If I came into a pot with K3 (and, yeah, I did that just as I did with AK, AA, or any other hand), and a three appeared on the flop, I never chased whirlwinds by going any further and folded then and there. I do confess to hanging around with K3 at first, if a king came on the flop as the top card on the board, but I doubt that I did even that for more than a week or so after I took up the game. I was blessed with pretty good card sense and very quickly figured out the importance of the kicker that went with top pair, and thereafter if I held really weak pocket cards such as K3, I never went past the flop unless the flop hit me in at least two places: two threes, two kings, or a king *and* a three.

And if the foregoing sounds familiar, it ought to, because that's exactly the advice I gave in *Play Poker Like a Pigeon*. In that book I said that in order to throw your opponents off as to your actual poker skills, you should come into just a few pots in early position with really crappy hands. If the flop hits you in at least two places and you get to proudly exhibit your 10-3 or worse while dragging the money, then everyone at the table will label you a sucker, which is exactly what you want them to do. So now you know where I got the idea, from my early beginnings as a Hold 'Em player when I won tons of money in a single month with some incredibly bad two-card hands.

And as for my stand that supposedly expert players often make worse plays than I ever thought about making as a nineteen-year-old, consider the "expert" manner of dealing with AK, supposedly one of the strongest hands in Hold 'Em: **The most overrated hand in Texas Hold 'Em is AK, because even so-called expert players often misplay the hand terribly. In a game with multiple players seeing the flop, AK is better than other nonpaired two-card hands only because if the flop hits AK, the hand assumes a commanding lead. The problem comes when the flop totally misses AK and hits one of the other pocket hands at the table. When that happens, even good players will often draw at overcards when holding AK— when they wouldn't dream of doing so with KQ or any other two cards—even though they have only six possible wins left in the deck, and the odds are strong that even if they catch an ace or a king they're going to lose the pot anyway. As I've harped on before, AK does not merit an automatic pre-flop raise in limit Hold 'Em. The main purpose for pre-flop raises is to eliminate the competition, and where you hold AK in late position, every player who's already called the blind will call the raise as well, and the only thing you're doing here is tipping off the others that you have two big cards in your hand. In early position you should raise with AK, because you might knock out some players who haven't yet acted on their hands, but in late position you're better off lying behind the lick log occasionally with AK—and I only say "occasionally" because it's never a good idea to play the same hands in the same way in the same position *every single time*, because if you do you'll be exhibiting a tell—and then if the flop should hit you, you'll**

**win a much bigger pot than you would if you'd raised be-
fore the initial three cards had appeared on the board.**

The jack-five that I picked up in my very first Hold 'Em
hand, of course, doesn't fit anyone's description of primo pocket
cards, and even as a novice I had enough sense that I would've
pitched jack-five unless the flop had hit me in two places. But
the flop hit me big-time and I won the pot, and from there I
embarked on the longest consecutive winning streak that I've
ever experienced in all my years of playing poker; I didn't know
it at the time, but the game that Steve had introduced me to
featured some of the best limit poker players in the world, all
of whom tore at their hair and rolled their eyes as my winning
ways went on and on. My play during that period was god-awful,
just as you'd expect from a nineteen-year-old novice Hold 'Em
player, but no one could've convinced me that I was anything
other than a totally brilliant poker prodigy. And today, every time
I see some fresh-faced youngster winning a fortune at the WSOP
in spite of some very bad play, I feel serious twinges of sympa-
thy, because I've been there. People on incredibly goofy winning streaks can play any two cards and walk on water; it wasn't
until about a year later that my cards cooled off to near-normal
temperature and I finally began to learn to play the game. As it
was I began my sophomore year in college with wads of cash in
my pockets, which heightened my popularity among the coeds,
and assured me that I wouldn't have to rub any more football
players' asses, because I could always slip another manager or
student trainer a ten spot to take my place manning the ultrasound.

And even though my dumb-lucky success at the poker table
had me convinced that I was the best card player since Hoyle,
I didn't play in the backroom pro-level Hold 'Em game again
until the following summer. There were a couple of reasons for
my abstinence; first of all, there was the football manager's gig

that took up all my afternoons and a lot of my evenings, and then there were the jockstraps' game and the Phi Delts' game, both of which were back in full swing once the fall semester began. I continued to live in the apartment with Steve; since we weren't running the poker game any longer he did require that I come up with my half of the rent, which due to my incredible luck during the summer's final month I had no trouble doing.

My sophomore year flashed by, and when summer came around I didn't bother applying for my old job changing truck tires. I would simply pick up a few thousand dollars more in the ten-and-twenty Hold 'Em game, just as I had the previous year, and by the time fall rolled around I'd be flush with cash once more. The first time I came to the old professionals' game I actually thought I might be barred because of my previous summer's winnings, and I breathed a sigh of relief when the players welcomed me with open arms and glad hands and whatnot. Little did I know. I envisioned a summer by the pool by day and at the poker table by night and never doubted for an instant that I'd have money to burn.

But, of course, I was dead wrong. Since the plan had worked out so well the summer before, I kept on with my strategy of seeing every flop, but for some reason I could no longer beat the AAs and KKs and whatnot and my jack-fives were now seeing something like two kings and a deuce on the flop, just as I deserved. Within just a few weeks my bankroll had shrunk to the point that one day I actually called the Firestone store and asked how they were fixed for tire changers. The manager told me that all of his summer positions were filled, which was probably just what I deserved as well.

To make matters worse, I'd lost contact with Steve. I knew he hadn't been playing any poker, because I'd been frequenting the games where he usually hung out, at the jockstrap dorm, the Phi Delt house, and the illegal backroom game on the east side of town. Officially he was still sharing the apartment with me and his clothes still hung in his closet, but I hadn't seen him in person since the beginning of summer. I suppose he could've been coming and going at night, while I was out at the poker game, but I'd seen no dirty towels or wet shower walls as evidence that he'd been there. Since I'd now come up with a case of the shorts I wanted to see about running the same game that we had had the previous summer, but I couldn't do it without him. The stamped clay chips were his and so were the couple hundred decks of diamond back Bicycle cards that were in his closet. Toni hadn't been around either, and I had no idea how to get in touch with her. I suppose she had her own place to live, but since she'd spent most of the previous year sleeping in Steve's bedroom I had no idea where her place might be. I was really sort of at the end of my rope. I had enough money to play in the poker game one or two more times, and after that it was Tap City for me.

So one warm night I put five hundred bucks in my pocket and made my way to the ten-and-twenty poker game. As far as I was concerned, it was do or die. The men in the game looked glad to see me. I didn't blame them for feeling that way. It wasn't the last time I'd play poker on case money, but on the occasions in later life that I've carried my bottom dollars to poker games, I was a pro-level player and a favorite to win. But the first time that I risked my last five hundred playing poker, I had just turned twenty years old, was very new to the game called Hold 'Em, and was going up on short money against a game that was as tough as any you'll find at the Bellagio today. In other words, the odds were heavily against me.

I had finally admitted to myself that my see-every-flop strategy wasn't the way to go, but I hadn't a clue as to the correct way to right the ship. The one saving thing I'd learned was to watch the really good players and try to follow their example; up to now my role model had been Steve, but he wasn't around, so I had to pick out someone else in the game to copy. I got very lucky; the player I decided to emulate was and is one of the three finest limit Hold 'Em players I've ever run across. I think I picked him because, even though he was six or seven years older than I was, he was the second-youngest player in the game by more than a decade. I suppose I'd better give him a name just as I gave one to Steve, so let's call him Don.

Don had grown up around gambling, and aside from being the most rock-solid player in a game populated by rock-solid players, he was also one of the game runners. The other game runner was the biggest illegal bookmaker there was in a city crawling with illegal bookmakers, and his only real interest in running the poker game was in meeting a lot of people who had sports-betting habits on which he could capitalize. In addition to running the poker game and being involved in the book-making operation, the guy owned a we-tote-the-note car lot that was really just a front for his poker and sports-betting operations. Occasionally, the Big Bookie played in his own ten- and twenty-dollar limit poker game, but with many thousands on the line in football bets every week from August until the end of January, he had little interest in the piddling sums he could win or lose at poker and was pretty much throwing his money away when he did play. Not so with Don. Don played tight but aggressive Hold 'Em, and after many hours with him at the table, I can honestly say that I've never seen the guy make a mistake. He is also a world-class gin player. In later years he was to join a country club, become a fair-to-middling golfer, and make his living off the club members for many years to come. The last I heard he was still at the same country club playing golf, poker, and gin every day and winning most days, and he's one of the very few limit card players I've known who've actually become wealthy at the game. I didn't know all of this when I picked Don to serve as my role model at the poker table, but I couldn't have found a better guy to copy anywhere in the world. Blind hogs and acorns, and all that jazz.

I don't want to give the impression that Don took me under his wing, because that wasn't the case at all. Pros are there strictly to win your money along with everyone else's they can manage, and there is no room among serious poker players for buddy-buddying around. I've now known Don for forty years. I don't run into him nearly as often as I used to, when I played at the same country club that he did for four or five years, but when our paths cross today we're cordial and that's about the size of it. If he's found a game with a number of weak players as regulars, he wouldn't cut me in on that action for all the tea in China, nor would I cut him in if the situation was reversed. We have a mutual respect for each other. If he dies before me, I won't be recruited for pallbearer duty, and neither will he if I'm the first to go.

But I'm still grateful for the period forty years ago when I used Don as a role model. Although he never gave me any tips, I learned more by observing his play than I could've ever picked up if he'd been trying to teach me. There's another lesson here: in going from poker game to poker game you'll be amazed at how few players pay attention to what's going on around them. They play their own games and only theirs. If you really want to improve your poker, keep up with which players are regular winners and pay close attention to their style of play. That's a better lesson than you'll get from any book, including this one.

So as I sat there in the ten-and-twenty game with my last half yard in front of me in the form of poker chips, I made up my mind to watch Don's play and try to copy his style as best I could. Every time he played a pot I paid close attention to (1) the hand he showed down at the end in relation to his position relative to the button; (2) the number of pots he played altogether; and (3) situations that seemed to prompt Don to call, raise, or fold. I learned things from watching Don that I believe to this day saved my career as a player, but, more importantly, I picked up hints from his demeanor and lifestyle that were more valuable than any playing tip.

As for the two-card hands he showed down at the end, well, I didn't see any jack-fives or anything similar, which confirmed the fact that my see-every-flop strategy was all wet, but since I only saw his cards when he'd played pots all the way through, it was hard to pick up on which two-card starting hands he would or wouldn't play. I didn't know position play from the West Coast Offense, but I couldn't help noticing that the closer he sat to the dealer, the more often he'd look at the flop. In the small- or big-blind position he would take a perfunctory glance at his hand, but with the exception of the times he had the big blind and no one raised before the flop, I don't think I ever saw him look at the first three cards to hit the board. It would be a number of years before Sklansky's Hold 'Em book would define the importance of position, though I'm glad that I picked up on position play through experience and not through reading a manual, because the strategy is more ingrained than when learned through a book— not nearly so much "What do I do here?" while squinting to read from Sklansky, but more instinctive play. Whatever it is I know about position I first learned from watching Don. And even though he played in very few pots, when he did come in to see the flop he played very aggressively. Checking and then calling didn't seem to have a place in Don's bag of tricks; it was from him that I first picked up on the strategy of before-the-flop raises in late position merely to chase the dealer and steal the button.

But much more important than Don's style of play was his demeanor in general. Nothing seemed to rattle him; no horrible beats (and he suffered as many of those as anyone), no amount of verbal abuse from other players (and if you don't know what I'm talking about here, just go to your nearest poker parlor and observe a few so-called poker experts while they're on extended losing streaks), *nothing.* When someone drew out on him he merely smiled; said, "Nice hand"; and tossed his cards away. He was a gentleman at all times and in all situations. I will absolutely guarantee you that if you can maintain a steady demeanor while those around you are cursing and throwing cards and whatnot, you will have a leg up on the competition that's more effective than any playing strategies can ever be. And if this sounds easy, believe me that it isn't; if Vatican insiders started a Hold 'Em game, members of the pope's entourage would have to stuff cotton in their ears in order to shut out the things that the pontiff himself might yell at the top of his lungs.

Another tribute to Don: The extensive chapter in my first book about computing odds in Hold 'Em had nothing to do with anything I picked up from him. The poker-playing community is alive with court holders, people who like nothing better than to spout off their knowledge of odds and whatnot to anyone who will listen. In all the years I've known Don, I've never heard him quote a single odd, declare how many "outs" (wins) a player has left in the deck, or make any comment about his own or anyone else's chances of winning a pot. Really smart Hold 'Em players refer to the practice of continually spouting off this odd or that odd as "wising up the suckers," and while the term might be a bit crude it happens to hit the nail on the head. If you have an advantage over another player because of your knowledge of odds, then *why educate the person and thus lose your advantage?* As for me, while emulating players like Don immensely helped me to develop my playing skills, the knowledge I have of poker odds I can attribute to the court holders. May their number increase, especially in games where I currently play.

And, by the way, watching Don and listening to the court

holders didn't turn me into an expert overnight; that process takes years. And my five hundred bucks? That first session where I made up my mind to become a good Hold 'Em player didn't make a winner out of me, but I did manage to lose less than I had been losing. I think I went home that night with around four hundred bucks, and I also seem to recall that I booked winners the next three or four times that I played, but there's no guarantee that as you increase your skills you will suddenly become a winner. Skillful play will make poker a profitable venture over the long haul, but any short-term success or lack of it is in the luck of the draw.

And (also by the way) this is as good a time as any to revisit my old buddy Steve, who when last heard of had pulled a disappearing act along with his girlfriend, Toni. I went through an entire summer and half of my third college year without ever laying eyes on the guy, though his belongings remained stashed in the apartment's bedroom closet. He paid no rent after his disappearance, so I had to finance the apartment on my own—which I managed to do by running a once-a-week poker game, just as I would've wanted to do if Steve had stayed put. Around the middle of the fall semester, I reasoned that if I had to pay the entire rent it made no sense for me to keep sleeping on the sofa, so I moved my gear into the bedroom. For a long time I worried intensely about Steve, but as the months rolled on I thought less and less about him. I did wonder if he'd died but supposed that if he had someone would've showed up to collect his things.

Then one cold January day about a week after Christmas break, I left campus and returned to the apartment to find— *boom!!*—Steve sitting on the couch surrounded by his stuff: his clothes, his portable stereo, and about fifty 45-rpm records. Prominently missing from his belongings were his chips and cards, which were still in the bedroom, and which I'd been using in my weekly game. I sat down, weak-kneed with shock, in a chair across the coffee table from him. He was thin to the point of emaciation, and his look was taut and drawn.

"Where . . . where the hell you been?" I finally said.

"I've been on many journeys," Steve said.

Surely this was a joke. I waited for the punch line. Steve maintained his grim expression. This story is hard to believe, I know, but it happened.

"I have walked through the Valley of the Shadow of Death," Steve said.

I nervously laughed. I wondered if Steve might suddenly build a fire to dance around, in order to bring rain or something. I said, "You find your chips and cards back in the closet?"

"I have no more use for those things," he said. "They are yours."

Always before Steve had been a regular guy—a very cool, handsome, with-it regular guy and a cut above the average jockstrap, but a regular guy nonetheless—but now he spoke in sort of an evangelist's dialect and his eyes were wild. If a time machine had materialized and suddenly whisked him off to another era, I couldn't have been more surprised. I tried to say something—anything—to bring back the Steve I knew and loved. "What's happened to Toni?" I said. "I haven't seen her since you left."

"She was resistant to change," Steve said.

Christ, had he murdered her? Or, more importantly, was he about to murder me? I said, "Well, where is she?"

He beamed at me like Christ at the lepers. "She left me on one of the journeys."

Do tell. I knew only that I wanted the hell away from him. I stood. "Look, Steve, I gotta go meet some people." I'm sure my voice cracked.

He studied me intently. He reached inside his coat and produced a Bible with the Gideon emblem on the cover. "First, we have to talk."

I eyed the Bible suspiciously. "Maybe later," I said.

"We have to talk about Jesus," Steve said.

My shock was over with, and I began to get mad. This guy had run out on me and left me with twice the rent that I'd expected to pay. I stepped toward the door. "I don't want to talk about Jesus right now. I don't want to talk to you about anything. I've got business to take care of. As far as the rent you owe, we're even. I'm calling it even for the chips and cards."

"But the Lord sayeth," Steve said.

"Bye, Steve," I said and quickly left the apartment. I got in my car and drove for two hours or more. When I returned Steve was gone, and so were his belongings. I wasn't to see him again for years, and I sometimes wondered if I'd imagined the entire incident. But I hadn't, and the fact that a mutual acquaintance saw Steve some years later healing the sick in a tent revival confirmed that what I remembered was real. Steve was (1) deadly serious about his religion and (2) crazy as a loon.

Steve had to be the weirdest dude whom I've ever met playing poker. There are others who run him a close second, but, at that point in my life, Steve would have taken the prize.

6

Doc Nichols and the Two Fours

There were nine of us in the room tied up like goats, me and the boxer on one bed and three more players on the other bed, with four guys in the fetal position on the floor. Monkey One and Monkey Two had left us alone, it seemed like an hour ago, and I was beginning to wonder if the two thugs had left without saying goodbye. They'd taken everyone's money the second that last unlucky person had come through the door, so it would be no trick at all for them to fade off into the sunset without announcing their departure. They could be twenty miles away by now. Since our players carried a couple thousand dollars in cash on average, the take could be as high as twenty grand, not a bad afternoon's work for anyone.

I'd pretty well gotten the boxer calmed down, though he continued to mumble something about whipping some ass every once in a while, and it occurred to me that the ass that the boxer now wanted to whip might be my own. I turned on my side and offered him an encouraging grin. He blinked and looked away from me.

I decided that since I was the game runner, it should be up to me to go to the front of the apartment and see if the hijackers were gone. I scooted off the bed, got my feet under me, and stood, a pretty good trick with my hands cuffed behind my back. You should try it sometime.

As I took one hesitant step toward the hallway, the shotgun went off in the front room. The blast was deafening. Glass shattered and tinkled. I sat back down on the bed and looked helplessly at the ceiling. I was speechless with fear.

I got out of college, and no, they didn't have to burn the school down to get rid of me. I was on the dean's list, as a matter of fact, though if you ask me *which* dean's list, I won't tell you. I had a degree and even scored a pretty good job as a trainee with a well-known company. My starting salary was $450 a month, which, believe it or not, in 1962 was a bit above the norm for someone with a bachelor's degree.

After my third day on the job I dropped by the same back-room poker game where I'd been playing all during my time as a student, and in two hours of ten-and-twenty Hold 'Em I won a shade over five hundred bucks. The next day my boss asked me out to lunch and took me to a German restaurant. We did talk a little business, though I was too green an employee to contribute much to such a discussion, and the lunch eventually became a get-acquainted bull session. When Old Bossy asked me in a palsy-walsy tone what I did for recreation, I told him straight out that I was a poker player. At first he thought my hobby was great and even asked me if I'd like to join his Thursday night fifty-cent game. I told him that I didn't play that kind of poker, then went into too much detail about my activities the night before.

My boss's complexion seemed to darken as I spoke, and by the time I'd finished I'd seen the last smile I'd ever get out of the guy. He told me that backroom poker parlors were illegal—as if I didn't know—and that if word got around that one of his trainees was involved in such a game it could do a lot of damage to the company's public image. He told me that the "Old Man" took exception to anything that could hurt the company's standing in the community, and that if the "Old Man" got wind of me playing in an illegal poker game he'd have my job. I've learned in later years that the "Old Man" in corporate America gets the blame for a lot of his line managers' dictums, even though the "Old Man" has never heard most of his underlings' orders attributed to him, but at the time I believed I was hearing it straight from the horse's mouth. I slept on my boss's instructions, and then the next morning I phoned in my resignation.

To set the record straight: I really intended to go on from there and find a company to hire me that wouldn't object to my playing a little high-stakes poker when I wasn't on the job, and I actually called and set up some interviews. But then I booked four consecutive winners in the poker game during the following week, and with my pockets stuffed with the equivalent of four months' salary from the job I'd just quit, I simply lost interest. I was to remain unemployed for most of the rest of my life—without missing a rent payment or a meal.

I confess to being a really lousy employee, so shoot me, but let me fill you in on a little secret. Playing poker for a living is no lazy man's pastime, and it's a thousand times harder than having a job. The public in general doesn't see it that way, because the public only sees people on television who sit around glancing at, and then—most of the time—tossing away their pocket cards, and every so often scooping in a pot worth many thousands of dollars, and in between winning pots, telling jokes or having a therapist massage their shoulders. But hear this: the skill and discipline required for success as a poker player far exceeds that needed for any other profession you can name, and I'm not saying that just because poker became my chosen profession. In the twenty-first century, gambling is legal in about 90 percent of the country, but when I began playing poker for a living, virtually all card rooms were illegal, and the hazards involved were ten times more dangerous than those of today.

Since I'm not running for political office or interviewing for a position with any Fortune 500 companies, I can state without any personal risk that I'm one of the people who believe that certain vices should be legal, such as narcotics, prostitution, and gambling. I've been lucky enough to avoid becoming a dope fiend (though I have long abstained from alcohol because of a drinking problem, and I am certain that if I'd ever sniffed any cocaine I'd be a nose-candy slave), and I've never been a whorehouse customer (though I've got no quarrel with those who are), but through a long acquaintance with many forms of gambling I can state with confidence that I'm an expert on that particular subject. State and local laws against dope, whores, and gambling accomplish two things: (1) they put the operation of those vices in the hands of some really dangerous criminals, and (2) they make it possible for politicians and cops to have oodles of graft crossing their palms in return for permitting illegal activities to go on.

Today all it takes to become a professional poker player is to say that you are one, and if you are a really skillful player you can eke out a living simply by driving to your nearest casino poker parlor two or three days a week—or at least that's what I do, though I know some professionals who spend so much time at the tables that there is no room in their lives for anything other than poker. Once you're finished playing you need merely cash in your chips at the window and go on home, and your neighbors need not be any the wiser unless you want them to be. Today there's no real reason to keep your occupation a secret, because as long as you're playing where card rooms are legal, no one's going to look down his or her nose at you like people did in the old days.

Now, compare the foregoing with what professional poker players had to go through to earn a living in the early to mid-1960s. Back then casino gambling was legal in this country in only one state, Nevada, and Las Vegas had yet to appreciate the potential profits to be had in poker rooms. The mob-run casinos were strictly into craps and blackjack, with roulette and nickel slots around to keep the ladies occupied while their husbands blew their money at twenty-one and on the galloping dominos. What poker there was in Las Vegas was downtown in the sawdust joints (as opposed to the plush strip hotels that were known as "rug joints"), and one would have been hard-pressed to find a game on most nights with higher than one- and two-dollar limit.

Besides Nevada there were a few scattered states, such as California and Montana, where poker was the *one and only* legal form of gambling, but the laws in those states made it impossible for a pro to ply his trade. In California, draw poker was defined as a game of skill and stud poker was defined as a game of chance (and if you're thinking, *What the fuck?* that's exactly the same thing I thought the first time I had the rule explained to me), so the only game permitted in Gardena card houses was five-card draw, and the few times I sat in on those games the players were so tight that they made dead men look like free-spending party guys. In Montana, the highest play permitted was five-dollar limit, and no pot was allowed to exceed a hundred dollars, so once a hundred bucks was on the table the betting ceased and the hand was played out to a showdown. I knew a guy who had gone to Missoula and had had a weeklong winning streak, but in the end he'd won barely enough money for a plane ticket home. If a professional wanted to make a living he either had to find illegal backroom poker parlors or try to get an "in" to some well-heeled doctors' or lawyers' game, because those were the only places where the stakes were high enough to support him if he won. Backroom games were plentiful, but it was dangerous as hell to play in them.

I'll plot the dangers for you: The police were the smallest threat to the poker parlors, and almost no threat at all to the players who frequented those places, because (1) raids only came during election years, so the game runners could simply close up for a couple of months and avoid the battering ram that the cops used to break down the door to the joint; (2) while the cops generally arrested the game runners, they pretty much left the players alone (though the police did seize all the cash they found on the premises so that the game runners and players alike took a financial hit, but whether the money ever made it to the police evidence locker was never known); and (3) even if the police took the game runners to jail, the judge generally released them on their recognizance, and no criminal case could be made without testimony from someone to the effect that the game runners were raking the pot (simply playing poker at a private place has never been a crime in any jurisdiction that I've ever heard of). Since none of the players had any incentive to become stool pigeons, the case would get a little ink in the papers for a while, but the DA always dropped the charges once the election returns were in. During the 1960s and '70s, I was involved in the running of four different illegal poker games without suffering an arrest. I also played in countless other illegal games, and although I was present for six different police raids, I never received so much as a written citation.

So much for the long arm of the law. Cops were more of an irritant to poker games than a danger. Cheats were a different proposition.

Cheating was pretty common in old-time backroom poker parlors even though the game runners would've liked to have stopped it, because once cheated in a certain joint the victim wasn't likely to return. The problem was that a lot of the cheaters were people who would kill without blinking, and game runners were more afraid of the cheaters than they were concerned for their customers' well-being. One old game runner used to say, only half kidding, "I can always dig up another poker player, but this ass I'm sittin' on is the only one I'm ever gonna have."

Actually one could avoid most cheats by merely sticking to the limit games; cheating incidents normally occurred only once per session and the pots in limit poker just weren't big enough to make the chance of getting caught worth the cheaters' time. All cheating I've seen was designed to trap a certain player, and one hand of no-limit Hold 'Em was plenty sufficient to rob the mark of a tidy sum.

There were backroom games in just about every major American city in those days, and every poker parlor I ever saw had pretty much the same setup: one or two tables devoted to ten-twenty- or fifteen-thirty-limit games, with the big no-limit table in its own private room hosting action only once or twice weekly. Today all casino card rooms, and nearly all illegal backroom games, employ house dealers, and that practice eliminates nearly all cheating. But when I started out, the deal passed around the table from player to player, and other than to come by and "take time" on the hour and half hour, the game runners stayed in the background. The very first time I ever sat in on a no-limit poker game, one of the old-timers told me, deadpan, "Now, if you get caught cheatin', son, you gotta sit out a hand." After a few seconds of stony silence, everyone at the table burst out laughing, and at the time I thought I'd just heard a local joke, so I joined in the merriment. But with forty-plus years of observation to look back on, I'm not so sure that the guy was kidding.

As for the methods of cheating, let's first eliminate the card mechanics. Those people existed, of course, and through the years I've known a few. Titanic Thompson's son Tommy, who when last heard from had joined forces with my old buddy Steve in finding Jesus and had become a full-time preacher, could deal out a series of draw poker hands while putting four kings in one hand, four queens in another, four aces in a third, and four jacks in a fourth, and you could look right at him as he cheated you and not find a thing suspicious in the way he handled the cards. Charles Harrelson, actor Woody Harrelson's father, was a mechanic of sorts, albeit a clumsy one, and performed most of his manipulations against tablefuls of drunks who couldn't have recognized cheating if a buzzer had gone off whenever Charles slid one off the bottom. Second dealers and card mechanics were generally used in blackjack games when the house needed a hot player cooled off, and card manipulation wasn't much good in Hold 'Em, because of the infinite number of combinations that players could use to make hands and the unpredictable number who'd stick around to see the flop. In other words, even if the mechanic gave the mark two kings while slipping two aces to himself, when multiple players other than the mark stayed in the pot to see the flop, the mechanic might find his aces losing to a straight or flush and the mark's money going into pockets that the mechanic hadn't intended it to.

The most popular method of cheating in Texas Hold 'Em was called cold decking, a highly effective ploy that didn't require any manipulation skills. Cold decking was a team effort, with a house man, a couple of players in the game, and a comely drink waitress in on the scam, and it worked like this: Whenever the mark looked fat and happy enough to be off his guard, the house man would go in the back and "stack" a deck, arranging the cards so that both the mark and the dealer would pick up monstrous betting hands. Then the dealer would shuffle as always and offer the cards for a cut. Once the deck was cut and ready to deal, the conspirators would go into action; the drink waitress would sidle up to the mark and ask him if he wanted a drink, often bumping him with a generous hip and showing him plenty of cleavage, while the other players in on the scam would offer the mark a string of gee whizzes about how well the mark was playing, all designed to distract the mark while the house man slipped the stacked deck to the dealer and pocketed the deck that had previously been in play. By the time the mark returned his attention to the game, the dealer would already be putting out the hand.

Cold decking usually worked to a tee. After the mark had lost his money, usually to a higher full house (the most popular stack had the dealer getting two tens and the mark getting two nines, having the flop come 10,9,2, and then have Fourth and Fifth Streets produce what seemed to the mark to be two perfect threes), he always suspected that he'd been had but was powerless to do anything about it. It's always mathematically possible for the mark's bad luck to be merely the luck of the draw, and that's what the cheats would all swear to have happened even as they headed for the back room to split up the mark's money.

There is one famous-among-old-time-poker-guys instance of the cold-decking plot backfiring, one that created a new name for a hand. Nicknames for certain card combinations are common in Hold 'Em. The two-card hand of 10-2 is called Doyle Brunson, because Brunson won the final hand at the WSOP with 10-2 two years in a row. Q10 is called Everett Goolsby, after an old-time Texas gambler (though I'm not sure why this is, since I've played a lot of poker with Goolsby and don't believe that he's any more likely to come in a pot with Q10 than he is K2 or any other combination), and two kings is called Cowboy Wolford, for reasons just as nebulous. A guy named Rich McComas has compiled hundreds of named Hold 'Em hands that you can review at www.holdemsecrets.com/handnamesa.htm. However, I've been over the list from A to Z and can state (1) that I've never heard of most of the hands listed even though I've played Hold 'Em regularly for two-thirds of my life, and (2) that McComas has failed to list one of the most famous hands of all—the Texas Hold 'Em hand of 44, which is called the Doc Nichols Hand.

Doc Nichols didn't really live to be older than God, though at times it seemed that he was going to. He was in his seventies the first time I sat down across the poker table from him, in 1964, and more than twenty years after that he still occupied a regular seat in the limit game at the Amvets Club on Dallas's Lower Greenville Avenue. Not only was Doc acquainted with every famous poker player in the world, but he'd played in games with many of their fathers. The following story might put things in better perspective for you: Once upon a time I was in Las Vegas during WSOP time, and I ran into Doc outside the Sombrero Room in the lobby of Binnion's Horseshoe. The Sombrero Room featured the only real Tex-Mex menu west of Amarillo at the time, and the customers would line up for hours waiting for tables. At the time, Doc Nichols was in his mid to late eighties, thin as a razor with a topping of snow-white hair, his bearing ramrod straight, his high-pitched voice faintly cracking with age. Doc was seated at an empty blackjack table and I was leaning against the banister rail. As we stood there, Becky Binion came along pushing her father Benny in a wheelchair. When Benny saw Doc Nichols, he had Becky wheel him over to where we were. Benny held out his arms and Doc leaned over to give him a hug.

Benny wasn't quite an invalid—though within a very few years he wouldn't be able to get around without a walker—and on this occasion he was in a wheelchair because he'd injured his knee. He was a Dallas native who'd migrated to Las Vegas in 1951; before his relocation he'd headed up virtually all of Dallas's gambling operations from his office in the University Club downtown on Commerce Street. I knew who Benny was but had never met him, and when Doc Nichols introduced me I was tongue-tied with awe. Benny winked at me and, pointing at Doc, said, "You're in good company here, son. Mr. Doc Nichols, he helped teach me the ropes when I was a kid."

I mean, Doc Nichols went *way back*, okay?

All of which leads up to the story of "The Hand." I don't think I've ever run across anything as odd as the relationship between old-time high-stakes poker players, and Doc's version of The Hand does plenty to back up my puzzlement. The Hand happened years before I first laid eyes on Doc Nichols. According to him, the main players (in other words, the conspirators who arranged to cold deck him) were Cowboy Wolford, Sailor Roberts (yet another poker Hall of Famer), a drink waitress named Scott Anna Moore, and the highest player of 'em all back then, a Dallas gambler named Legs Greenlease.

And here's the reason I find the relationship between all of these people so odd: at the time I met Doc, *he was still playing poker regularly with two of the guys whom he claimed cheated him* (Legs Greenlease was dead), and the drink waitress in the joint where Doc was playing every day was none other than Scott Anna Moore. I've always felt that if someone cheated me and I knew it, at the very least I'd never sit down to play with that person again, but the old-time gamblers' attitude seemed to be, okay, he got me, so next time I might get him.

Scott Anna's beauty had faded some by the time I met her, but you could tell by looking at her that in her day she was something else, and as Doc told the story I pictured her in shorts and a halter running drinks back and forth as the three no-goods plotted in the bathroom. Doc was the big winner in the game (it's always the big winner who gets cold decked, by the way), and the deck was stacked to give Doc two fours on the deal while Cowboy Wolford picked up a pair of fives. Sailor Roberts was acting as house man, so it was he who ran up the deck back in the john. When the time came, Legs Greenlease distracted Doc with a joke, Scott Anna bumped Doc with her hip and showed him plenty of boob, Sailor and Cowboy switched the decks, and the scam was on. The flop came out perfectly as planned, with both a five and a four on the board, and the deck primed and ready to deliver two perfect sixes on Fourth and Fifth Streets. After the flop, Doc made a token bet, Cowboy gave him a token raise, and then Doc shoved his entire stack into the center of the table. Cowboy called quickly and, with both players all in, both Doc and Cowboy exposed their hole cards. Then Cowboy prepared to deliver the two running sixes that would do Doc Nichols in.

There is always a time during the cold-deck scam when the mark realizes that he's been taken, but it's nearly always too late for him to do anything about it. In this case, Doc knew better than to start tossing out accusations because the others would deny everything, and Doc would have no way to prove that they were lying. Doc also knew that with the deck prestacked, there wasn't a chance in hell that any card would come on the turn or the river that would help him. In fact, the case four was the only card that could save him.

Out of sheer desperation Doc took the only action that could possibly turn things in his favor: he called for a cut. It was his right to do so, just as it was every player's right to cut the cards in any pass-the-deal poker game (this isn't true in casino games where there's a house dealer, by the way, because the house is smart enough to know that once it allows cutting the cards there are players who would want a cut before every single card came off the deck, and then other players would ask for a recut, and the hand might never end). Cowboy couldn't deny the cut without blowing the cold-deck scam all to hell, so he offered the deck to Doc.

And lo and behold, Doc Nichols cut the cards and the fourth four appeared on Fifth Street. The good guy won and the bad guys got clobbered in this case, though it's the only cold-deck scam I've ever heard of that failed.

Is the story true? Well, we'll get to the veracity of old gamblers in general, but I can say that I've played in games where Doc held forth and told the story with both Cowboy and Sailor sitting at the table listening to him, and I never heard either of them deny that it happened. There's no doubt in my mind that Doc believed that the incident really happened, but it could be a case of his having told the story so often that it seemed real. There's always the argument that any self-respecting cold-deck artists would have had the fourth four in the deck buried in the bathroom trash can, but since cheaters are seldom the brightest bulbs around, it's quite possible that doing away with the one remaining four never occurred to them. But nothing changes the fact that the Hold 'Em hand of two fours is the Doc Nichols Hand and always will be.

I could go on for hundreds of pages with stories of cheaters past and present—in fact, those old cheat stories might well make another book someday—but we're here to merely touch on the subject as it related to the poker life before the countrywide advent of legal casino games. Just remember that if you're a serious poker player you'll run into people you've heard of from time to time, and that the better known the poker player, the closer the eye one should keep on that player. But before we move on, please indulge me for just a few more pages. There is one more story I want to relate in order to emphasize the overall trustworthiness of the gamblers of yesteryear. The story involves the most famous gambler who ever lived, none other than Titanic Thompson.

There's no poker in this tale, even though the lesson it teaches is right in line with our subject matter. In the mid-1960s, Alvin

C. Thomas, better known as Titanic Thompson, became a regular hanger-on at Dallas's Tenison Park Municipal Golf Course. Ti was in his seventies then and a much more mellow man than the guy we'd all heard of and read about. For four or five years he used Tenison Park as his home base, jumping off into poker games and crap games in the surrounding communities from time to time, but mostly holding forth at Tenison daily, where he taught us some of the damnedest dice and card propositions ever heard of. Ti actually had a system for beating casino craps, a system as mathematically sound as 2 + 2 = 4, a system that I saw him work in Las Vegas and one that I'd be glad to explain to anyone who has the right price to pay for it. There's a lot of ink given to blackjack counters and the MIT Blackjack Team and all that jazz, but please note that casinos exhibit their real concern over the counters' advantage by (1) dealing all of the cards faceup to make it easier for the counters to count, and (2) selling books and pamphlets explaining the counting system in the gift shops that surround the casino floor. You'll never find a book detailing Titanic Thompson's craps system, and I doubt that there are ten living people who are familiar with it. Most old blackjack card counters think that Edward Tharp really screwed the pooch for everyone when he published *Beat the Dealer* back in the 1960s, because once the system became available to the public, the casinos set up defenses that made counting cards in blackjack totally ineffective. Ti's craps-beating ploy has a huge advantage over card counting, in that casino bosses are so smug about their dice percentages that even if you explained Ti's system to them in detail, they'd hoot you out of their offices and tell you to go right ahead with your system on their casino floor. The last time I employed the system was just last month in a Shreveport, Louisiana, casino while I waited for a seat in a poker game. I won. Over the past forty years I've won at craps with Ti's system 90 percent of the time I've used it.

But enough; this story isn't about craps systems. It's not about golf, either, though the events described happened on a golf course. I suppose that in order to put this story into perspective, I should briefly explain about me and golf. A room full of poker players is also a room full of golfers of one skill level or another, and I'm no exception. I look on poker as a business. Golf, however, is my passion, the brass ring I've never been able to grab, the source of my life's frustrations. On the day I die I'll still be searching in vain for golf's hidden secrets. And don't worry, I'm never gonna find them.

Tenison Park is the course where Lee Trevino played most of his golf at the time, as a total unknown and where the man who was, quietly and in the background, golf's greatest hustler hung out every day. (Ti tried to get Lee to go on the road with him as a hustler, but Lee declined, and in 1967, he finished fifth as a qualifier in the U.S. Open, went on tour, and has never regretted the decision.) Golf's greatest hustler was a small, nondescript man named Dick Martin, who among other things was the legendary Johnny Moss's moneyman, the guy Moss looked up when he was tapped out for poker funds. During the last half of the 1960s, Dick Martin used Titanic Thompson like a personal ATM.

Okay, we'd heard all the stories just as you have, how Ti won bets on the distance to certain cities by going out at night and moving the mileage marker signs, how Ti once won a bet that he could drive a golf ball a mile by performing the stunt on frozen Lake Michigan with a high wind behind him, how Ti could toss cards underneath a door into a hat, how Ti could throw a key into a lock, and on and on and on. I personally look on all of the foregoing as pure unadulterated bullshit, right up there with Paul Bunyan and the Blue Ox Babe. Questions that came to mind when I heard those tales: (1) When riding in a car with Titanic Thompson, known to be the greatest sucker-proposition man in the world, and passing a highway sign that says it's fifty miles to Oklahoma City, when Ti offers to bet a thousand dollars that he can get to Oklahoma City in thirty minutes, who the hell but a retard is going to accept that proposition? (2) And who the hell, with a fifty-mile-an-hour wind whistling up his ass, and with no idea how far from shore the ice thinned out to where he'd fall through the crust into the lake, chased that golf ball across Lake Michigan in subzero temperatures to measure how far it had gone? And as for the card-tossing and key-throwing fables, I'll only offer this: One afternoon at Tenison Park several of us got up a pool to bet Ti that he could neither throw a key into a lock nor toss a card underneath a door into a hat, the proposition being that if he was successful at either one he'd win the money. Ti declined, and with the pile of money on the table, I believe with all my heart that if he could've really performed either trick, he would've taken us on. But even when we offered to lay him two to one for the money, he wouldn't so much as try.

Okay, I'm through venting, and I'll further state that some of the antics attributed to Ti no doubt really happened. It's undisputed that Titanic Thompson was part of a group who cheated Arnold Rothstein, the 1919 World Series Black Sox fixer, out of thousands in a New York City poker game, and that Ti became a witness in the murder trial after someone—the police charged gambler George McManus with the crime, but McManus was acquitted at trial, and many believed that mobster Dutch Schultz actually arranged the hit—popped Rothstein over his failure to come up with the poker money he'd lost. You'd have to agree that Ti was no stool pigeon; trial transcripts have him giving his name and then taking the Fifth Amendment fourteen times before the DA gave up questioning him. So while Ti actually had a colorful history, there are so many tales about him that couldn't possibly be true that, in telling about Ti's life, chroniclers simply don't know where the facts end and the fiction begins. When it comes to Ti, I prefer to tell only of events that I witnessed with my own two eyes. What follows is the one I've been leading up to.

Before the story can be completely told there's another character who needs introduction, a short, round, bald guy who generally played Sancho Panza to Ti's Don Quixote, only this guy's name was Jimmy. Wherever Ti went, there Jimmy was as well, and rumor had it that Jimmy was the ringer of a caddy whom Ti would run in to play the guy whom Ti had just lost to by a couple of strokes. Ti would bet the guy that his caddy could beat him, and Jimmy would then shoot 65 or so when the heat was on. There was a another rumor that Jimmy was the guy who went out at night and moved the "50 Miles to Oklahoma City" sign twenty-five miles closer to town so that the next day Ti could bet his mark a grand that he could drive from the sign to Oklahoma City in thirty minutes. Personally I'm having neither of those stories. One day when Jimmy didn't know I was watching I saw him hitting golf balls at a driving range, and I don't recall him ever getting one off the ground for a distance of more than fifty yards, so I don't picture Jimmy as a golf hustler; and since Jimmy was so overweight that he could barely waddle, I don't picture Jimmy as the sign mover, either. I have Jimmy pegged as, perhaps, the guy who went into the john to stack the cards when Ti had the cold-deck scheme on, but that's just me, and if Jimmy reads this, and if he was secretly hustling me on the day I saw him topping golf balls right and left, then I apologize (but I'll still bet Jimmy that he can't shoot 65, and lay him six to one). Whatever his role, every time Ti played golf, there was Jimmy, tagging along in a golf cart by himself. I guess it's possible that Jimmy could've been Ti's ball-kicker-outer-from-behind-a-tree, and because the gang at Tenison Park had seen such shenanigans before, they made Jimmy keep his cart in sight when they were gambling against Ti on the golf course.

Anyhow, onward we go. Titanic Thompson had been a Tenison hanger-on for only a couple of months, and the golf hustlers weren't sure how to figure the guy. On showing up at the golf course out of the blue one day, Ti had introduced himself all around, and there were even a few of the Tenison crowd—a big-time bookmaker named Ace Darnell and all-time great golf hustler Dick Martin, to name a couple—who'd known Ti during their travels to other parts of the country. Ti surprised the gang by immediately joining the toughest golf game on the course— a game that had sent touring pros home COD on a regular basis— and betting high. The game included Dick Martin, who probably averaged about sixty-eight strokes a round at Tenison, and three or four other players whose skills were only slightly below Dick's.

The legend: Titanic Thompson was a fantastic golfer who could shoot par either left-handed or right-handed, and who had hustled both Sam Snead and Byron Nelson for tidy sums.

What I observed in person: Ti wasn't a bad golfer for a man in his seventies, but that's about the best you could say about his game during those years, and the Tenison crowd, having heard the same Paul Bunyan stories about Ti and his golf that you no doubt have, suspected that the guy was concealing his true game as he tried to get the betting stakes up higher. You could tell by the way Ti gripped the club and addressed the ball that he'd played a lot of golf, and the man was a dynamite chipper and putter, but his flexibility was so limited at that point in his life that he couldn't raise the club above waist level on his backswing, and I don't think I ever saw him hit a full shot that traveled as much as two hundred yards. If I were to handicap Ti in those days, I'd place his game at about a twelve, which is, of course, better than the average amateur, but nowhere near the skill level required to play in the company he was keeping. He never asked for any strokes, and the Tenison crowd, being the pack of vultures that they were, never offered any, and for a couple of months Ti lost big money on a daily basis and paid off in cash while the Tenison players, knowing that they were dealing with the legendary Titanic Thompson, kept a watchful eye and waited for the next shoe to fall. There was daily club-house chatter speculating on what scam the golf hustlers were about to fall victim to, but none ever emerged. There was some speculation about Jimmy, and the possibility that Ti might suddenly want Jimmy as his partner in the match, but the days wore on and on and Ti continued to lose, and if a plot involving Jimmy was about to hatch, there wasn't any indication of it.

The devil finally jumped up to challenge the Tenison gang one afternoon on the seventeenth hole, long par four, woods on the left up near the green (since the hustle wasn't a golf bet, the difficulty of the hole wasn't really a factor in the story, but remember the woods on the left, because they were to become a major player). I wasn't playing golf that day, but I was riding in a cart sitting beside Dick Martin, who'd been kind enough to let me have a piddling portion of his action. The gamblers were in a fivesome, with Titanic Thompson playing individually against each of the other four. On the seventeenth, all five players hit good drives, though Ti's was the shortest, as usual, and he'd hooked his ball so that even though it lay in the fairway, it was close to the left-hand woods. Dick kicked the cart into gear and the entire group motored off down the fairway.

Just short of where his ball lay, Ti threw on his brakes and leaned over to whisper something to Jimmy—Jimmy riding in the cart with Ti instead of solo in his own cart was unusual, and a circumstance that should have set off a few warning bells. As the other golf carts gathered round, Ti rose up in his seat and said to the group in general, "I'm tired as hell of losin' my money out here. I can't beat you-all on the golf course, but I'm wanting to lay a proposition."

The Tenison players exchanged looks that clearly said, "Aha, here it comes." Dick Martin nudged me with his elbow, then said to Ti, "What proposition is that, Titanic?"

"I got me a pistol in that golf bag, and I'm willing to bet a thousand dollars that if little Jimmy here carries a saucer fifty paces over in them woods and holds the saucer over his head, I can hit the saucer shootin' from the hip. If I make a mark on Jimmy, I lose. If I don't hit the saucer, I lose. A thousand dollars says I can do it." Ti reached in his pocket and exhibited a roll of bills held in a money clip.

The other gamblers grinned as one. This was the one they'd been waiting for; just as legendary as Ti's proposition bets was his skill as a pistol shot, and the Tenison regulars weren't about to fall for this one. A couple of the guys said, "No thanks," and two of the carts started to drive away.

Dick Martin said, "How big's this saucer you're aimin' to shoot at, Titanic?"

The two carts that had started to drive away came to a halt, and a couple of the gamblers cocked their heads in disbelief. Dick Martin was the guru of the gang, and many of them would make bets, sight unseen, if Dick was betting the same way. In other words, if Dick was willing to risk his money, the bet must be a lead pipe cinch. But, Christ, this was *Titanic Thompson* they were dealing with.

Ti climbed down out of his cart and nodded to Jimmy, who hustled around to stand behind Ti's golf bag. He unzipped one zipper and produced a standard white teacup-sized saucer, held it up for all to see, then dug back into the bag and pulled out a gun. I knew nothing about pistols in those days—and don't know much about them today—but this pistol's shape was so distinctive that even I could identify it as a WWI-vintage German Luger. Jimmy handed the pistol to Ti, who sighted down the barrel toward the woods.

Dick got out of our cart, approached Jimmy, and took the saucer. He turned the tiny glass plate around and around in his hands, peering at it on all sides, once tapping it against the ground. Finally, he nodded and returned the saucer to Jimmy. "You got you a bet, Titanic," Dick said.

And away Jimmy laboriously waddled, gasping for breath, his fat tail jiggling, until he stood in the shadow of the trees fifty yards away. He held the saucer high over his head.

Ti looked around at the crowd. "Anybody else takin' this action?"

The gamblers had a dilemma. They all knew that Dick bet on nothing but sure things. But they'd also known Dick for years and understood quite well that he was capable of "putting them in the tank"—prearranging the entire scenario so that Ti would hit the saucer dead center and win the bet, and then Ti and Dick would meet later at some secret location to split up the other gamblers' money. Finally, the Tenison crowd members shook their heads as one. "Ain't bettin' against no Titanic Thompson," one guy said.

"Suit yourselves," Ti said. He turned toward the woods and squinted at Jimmy. Ti held the Luger by his hip and spread his feet in quick-draw posture.

Dick said, "Hold it there, Titanic." He went over and took the pistol from Ti, then hit the release and pulled the clip from the handle. He examined the clip very carefully. Then he stuck Ti's clip in his pocket, pulled out a clip of his own, stuck the substitute into the handle slot, and banged the clip home with the heel of his hand. "Let's use these," Dick said. He handed the pistol back over.

Jimmy stood immobile fifty yards away. Ti looked dubious.

He looked at the pistol, then held it by his hip and spread his feet like Pat Garrett after Billy the Kid. Dead silence reigned.

Jimmy dropped the saucer; yelled, "Fuck no! Fuck no!"; and sprinted away through the woods. I swear to God, the guy could barely waddle, yet there he was moving along like a sprinter. He disappeared from sight over a rise.

Ti's shoulders sagged. He looked helplessly around him.

"That's a thousand you owe me, Titanic," Dick Martin said.

Ti mumbled something that sounded like, "I never got to shoot. Bet's off if I can't shoot at it."

"Okay, we'll see about that," Dick said. He jumped back into the cart beside me, hit the accelerator, and drove us over to the spot where Jimmy had dropped the saucer. Dick got out, looked around on the ground for a moment, then leaned over and picked something up. He held out what was in his hands so that I could see it; Dick was holding a white teacup-sized saucer that was shattered into four or five pieces. On his way into the woods, Jimmy had either broken the saucer or switched the shattered saucer for the whole one, and clearly the intent had been for Ti to shoot the pistol (which was loaded with blanks, as Dick's inspection of the clip he'd removed from the Luger was to prove), and then for Jimmy to simulate the saucer being hit and shattered so that Ti could collect a thousand bucks for his trouble. His problem was that Dick Martin already knew the trick and had been lying in wait for Ti. At some earlier time, Dick had searched Ti's golf bag and looked the pistol over and—surprise, surprise—had come up with a Luger clip of his own, only Dick's was loaded with real bullets.

Dick drove the cart over to where Ti stood and dropped the shattered plate on the ground at the famous gambler's feet. "I ain't taxing you nothing for trying to cheat," Dick said, "but you owe me a thousand and I aim to collect it."

Ti hemmed and hawed. He paced. He frowned. But he knew he had no face-saving choice other than to come across, and, finally, he counted out ten one-hundred-dollar bills and turned them over to Dick. The other Tenison gamblers, having turned down a chance to take the bet themselves, looked a little bit green around the gills.

The lesson? There is one, believe it or not. In dealing with "famous" gamblers—and this doesn't happen only on golf courses; the same sort of thing goes on in just about any venue where men are apt to risk money on the outcome of a game or the turn of a card—you must separate legend from what you know to be true and stick to your factual guns. The legend: Titanic Thompson was a man with a lightning-quick mathematical mind who used his knowledge of odds to always know which side to bet on. The truth: While Ti really did have a remarkable feel for the laws of probability, I never knew him to bet—other than on casino dice tables when he used his craps system—based on his odds figuring alone. In reality, Ti was a cheat with an uncanny knack for recognizing compulsive gambling problems, and he knew how to take advantage of those weaknesses in order to cheat people with them out of their money. If a man had to bet and couldn't help himself, Ti simply figured out a bet that the man couldn't win. He continually ran across people who had heard of him and who would give him action just so they could brag about having gambled with the famous Titanic Thompson. I had no such problem; since I'd watched the pistol-shooting fiasco from an up-close and personal standpoint, I never had any illusions about Ti's honesty, and any proposition he offered me I turned down without a second thought.

And since this book is about playing poker for profit, pay close attention to the following postulate as it relates to what we just learned about Titanic Thompson: **To eliminate all chance of being cheated, stick to the limit games; not even Ti would** cheat unless the amount at stake in a single proposition made the scam worth his time. Most poker players have this Walter Mitty dream of saying "All in" as they move their chips to the center of the table and won't heed this advice, so if you simply must try no-limit, and also must play with the so-called best—who, in reality, are only players who happened to be in a hand when the TV camera came rolling around—then you must also put the blinders on and play poker if you're going to have any chance of winning. This is difficult to do, but you'll have a great deal more success if you can shut out your awe of the celebrity and play your hand based on what you know to be the correct way regardless of who is sitting across from you. And in reality, famous no-limit poker players have no more skill than you, but certain ones do have access to more money. In no-limit poker, the player with the most chips in front of him or her has a tremendous advantage over the field; the mere fact that he or she can break any player at the table and the other players can't break him or her gives this player an almost insurmountable edge. Just watch Brunson (in a cash game, not some TV fiasco) and you'll see him keep adding to his stack until he has more chips than anyone else, regardless of the circumstances and whether he's winning or losing. Poker is lousy with something-for-nothing players, folks who want to risk, say, a hundred bucks with a chance to win millions if they should get lucky enough. But as long as your opponent can put a stack on the table bigger than yours, the inevitability will eventually strike home and the other person will draw out on you to win one big hand, after which you'll be headed home while the big-timer continues to play.

And I give the forgoing advice in full knowledge that you're going to ignore it, but you'll find that every successful big-time no-limit player (and I use the term "successful" loosely since even the "successful" no-limit players spend a lot of time scaring up a bankroll after they've lost their asses) isn't worried about how much he or she can lose but only concentrates on what he or she can win: Avoid no-limit poker like the plague, and if you must try no-limit or die from curiosity, under no circumstances get into a no-limit game in anything other than a legal, state-regulated card room. If you ignore the foregoing sentence the cheats are going to take your money. It is, however, your money, and no one can dictate how you go about spending it.

So much for the cheats. Next up the ladder in degree of danger to the pre-twenty-first century player came the hijackers. Poker game hijackers came in all shapes and sizes; many were players themselves with a case of the shorts while others were robbers by profession who recognized big-money poker games as primo pickin's—all cash and plenty of it, carried by gamblers who, when faced with the business end of a shotgun, would give up the money without a struggle, and who, because of the illegality of the game itself, would never call the police once the hijacking ended.

As scary as armed stickups might seem for the poker players, hijackers very seldom shot anyone; they came, showed their weapons, left with the money, and some even told the players whom they'd just robbed how long to wait before showing their faces once the hijackers had exited the building. I've even heard of hijackings where the robbers when asked would allow a tapped-out victim to keep twenty bucks or so for meal money. As a matter of fact, I've only heard of one shooting during a gambling hijacking, and the victim of the shooting wasn't a player but one of the hijackers themselves. The following is quite a tale.

You may recall that one of the alleged cold deckers on whom Doc Nichols turned the tables by cutting the fourth four out of the deck was a Dallas gambler named Legs Greenlease. Not only was Legs the biggest player in town and a consistent winner, but he was also the most hijacked man in America, bar none. By Legs's own estimate, he'd been held up over a hundred times. Not that Legs did much in the way of making himself less of a target. He was as flamboyant as they came, bragging to one and all about the amount of his wins, pulling out a roll of hundred-dollar bills whenever he paid for anything, including a tube of toothpaste at the drugstore. Local Dallas hijackers began to realize that robbing Legs was a bird's nest on the ground, not to mention that sticking a pistol in Legs's face was a whole lot less risky than robbing an entire poker game and worth a lot more money. Robberies became such old-hat propositions that Legs began to prepare for them; whenever he made a big win he assumed that someone would hold him up on the way home, so he always hid half his loot in a cigar box locked up in the trunk of his car. Half of Legs's bankroll was plenty to satisfy any hijacker, and it was also enough that robbers wouldn't start looking for more, torturing Legs for information in the process. As for the hijackers, they had Legs's address committed to memory, and sometimes when he played poker a robber would be waiting for him in his yard when he got home. Legs always suspected that someone connected to the poker game was tipping off the hijackers when Legs made a win, and then collecting a portion of the hijack proceeds, but he was never able to prove his suspicions. Personally, I think Legs was right on target; I knew most of the thieves he played poker with, and those guys when broke were capable of about anything.

October 31, 1957, was a Friday, a Halloween night with witches and goblins flitting about under a round harvest moon. Legs Greenlease left his house around sundown, kissing his wife at the door, then settling his lanky frame into the driver's seat of his white Cadillac ragtop and heading for the Oak Cliff section of town. It was big-game night at the VFW (almost all illegal poker rooms have a national organization as a front, the

Veterans of Foreign Wars and the American Veterans Association the most popular, followed closely by the Redman's Club), and the town was up to here with high players. Legs was one of the first to arrive, thus guaranteeing him a seat in the game. The game kicked off promptly at eight. By three in the morning, Legs was twelve thousand dollars ahead. He quit the game, collected his winnings, and headed for home. Before he got in his car he put half his money into his secret cigar box and locked the trunk. He made the drive to North Dallas keeping under the speed limit; he never picked up a tail in his rearview, and a half block from his house he thought he might, for once, actually make it home without having to turn any of his money over to a gunman.

He parked and left the car at a fast pace, making it halfway across his lawn before a masked gunman stepped out from behind a tree. The gunman pointed his weapon. "Okay, Legs, stick 'em up and lemme have it," he said. (Legs Greenlease was on a first-name basis with most of the hijackers in town; at times he even recognized their voices and knew who was robbing him, though he never publicly accused anyone for fear that the next time the hijacker might shoot him dead. And as for the hijacker's referral to the money as "it," well, being held up had become such a regular event in Legs's life that the robber no longer had to tell Legs what he'd come for.)

With a resigned sigh, Legs handed over six thousand dollars rolled up in a rubber band, then stood back with his hands raised. The hijacker said, "Thanks" (according to Legs Greenlease, the hijackers had gotten to know him so well that they often thanked him for cooperating), turned around, and started to leave.

Less than fifty feet away, a second masked gunman stepped out in the open and pointed his weapon at the first hijacker. The second guy said in a gravelly voice, "Put the money on the ground, you sonofabitch."

Legs stood there with his hands pointed skyward, puzzled. He looked first at one hijacker and then at the other. Apparently both men had received independent tips that Legs had made a win and was headed for home.

The first robber started to raise his hands just as Legs had done, but then suddenly dropped to one knee and fired off a shot in the general direction of the second hijacker. His aim was terrible; the bullet streaked harmlessly overhead.

The second hijacker pulled the trigger and shot the first guy through the heart. The first hijacker pitched over on his back, blood bubbling from between his lips.

The second robber stepped forward. His pistol hung by his hip. "Jesus Christ," he said, "I shot the guy."

Legs stood there with his hands up. He didn't say anything.

"I shot the fucking guy," the masked man said. He seemed in shock. Hijackers normally didn't have to shoot anyone, and it was obvious that this shooting was a first for the guy.

Ever nimble of wit, Legs lowered his arms. "Yeah, you did. You come in a car?"

The gunman nodded mutely. On the ground, the first hijacker had stopped breathing.

Legs said, "The guy was pulling a robbery. Tell you what— you want to leave, I'll see that nobody connects you to this."

The gunman spoke like a robot, "You'd do that?"

"Sure. You shot the guy who was robbing me. One good turn deserves another. Go on and haul ass. I'll take care of this guy." Legs pointed at the man on the ground.

The gunman said shakily, "Thanks." (I'm not making this up; Legs Greenlease told me that the guy thanked him. I was dubious, but Legs then stuck to his story through several rounds of questioning.) The gunman turned tail and sprinted away toward the street. In seconds a starter chugged, and then an engine caught and raced. Tires squealed as the robber drove away.

Legs was left alone with a dead man. His wife had heard the gunfire and stood cringing just inside the front door. Legs shooed her back inside; searched the corpse and retrieved his six thousand dollars; then grabbed the dead man under the armpits and, huffing and puffing, hauled the body over to his Cadillac. Moments later, the corpse locked in his trunk and the cigar box now on the front seat beside him, Legs drove to Trinity River-bottom and dumped the corpse, still wearing the mask, into a culvert. Then he went home and slept like a baby, and if anyone ever discovered the body, Legs didn't hear about it.

"Did you ever take off the mask and look at him?" I said to Legs nearly twenty years later.

Legs scratched his forehead. "What for?"

"Didn't you want to see who was robbing you? You might even have known him."

"Probably I did," Legs said. "But if I did know him, then I woulda felt obligated to tell his old lady or mother or somebody. Otherwise, he woulda been on my conscience. Better I didn't know. And the other guy?"

"The second hijacker," I said.

"Yeah," Legs said. "I didn't much want to know who the dead guy was. And the guy who shot him? I *really* didn't care who he was. Matter of fact, I woulda covered my ears if anybody'd tried to tell me his name."

Although Legs Greenlease was without a doubt the most hijacked man alive, and although he did witness the only known case of one hijacker shooting another hijacker who was in the midst of pulling a robbery, the one-after-another hijackings Legs experienced were isolated incidents and brought on for the most part by Legs's own flamboyant lifestyle. Every full-blown poker game robbery I've ever heard of went on without violence, so the overall situation was this: even though a poker player was unwise to go to any game with his entire cash assets in his pockets because of the possibility of hijackings, other than losing what money he'd brought to the game, the player was really in no danger of getting killed. Not that the foregoing information was much comfort with a shotgun pointed at one's head, but if the hijackees kept their cool and didn't give the robbers any trouble, they were sure to come out alive. So though I do rate hijackings as a serious danger to old-time poker pros, much more so than the police or the cheats, hijackings were nowhere near as dangerous to the players as the gangsters whom they played with on a daily basis. Now, those folks would kill you without batting an eye.

Illegal backroom poker games crawled with gangsters, and more than half the people who claimed to be professional poker players really were involved in other—often violent—types of crimes and merely played poker to pass the time when they weren't dealing dope, pulling robberies, or committing murders for hire. Knowing who was and wasn't dangerous to a player's well-being was an important part of the poker life, though poker game confrontations with gangsters sometimes couldn't be avoided, and it was an unfortunate part of the poker life back then that people occasionally died very young.

I'm not exaggerating any of this, and those who have taken up high-stakes poker more recently, and in essentially legal environments, don't really appreciate how lucky they are not to have to worry about such things as murders or—much more common than actual killings—assaults and muggings, which often landed the victim in the hospital. In many of those old games a player had two goals: (1) to win, and (2) to make it home in one piece with his winnings. If he had achieved both, he'd had one helluva good day.

This isn't a particularly pleasant part of the past to dwell on, but for one to really understand those poker players who went before the current crop, a couple of examples are in order. The first has to do with a game runner named Gene Trigg, who many years ago had the backroom game at the Amvets Club on Dallas's Lower Greenville Avenue. Gene ran afoul of the IRS—or, to be more accurate, local cops could never pin running an illegal poker game on Gene, so they sicced the Feds on him—and received a six-month stint in the federal lockup at Seagoville for tax evasion. Just before he reported to do his time he reached an agreement with a couple of thugs to the effect that they would run the game in his absence for 50 percent of the take, putting Gene's portion of the money aside for him to give him a nest egg once he hit the street.

The bond among thieves not being near as strong as is generally believed, the thugs proceeded to spend their own part of the take, Gene's part as well, and even more. They lived high, bought new cars and whatnot, thus depleting the cash available to the Amvets game, so some of the players weren't getting paid their winnings. And the thugs had a lot of nerve; when pressed to pay by players, they'd merely threaten mayhem, and the players were more than glad to go on their way unpaid.

Finally, Gene's release date came. He left the penitentiary around ten in the morning, made the thirty-mile trip from Seagoville to Dallas, and by one in the afternoon was back at his old post running the Amvets game. I happened to be in the joint that day, playing ten-twenty. I was surprised to see Gene, so I went over and shook his hand. I knew about the problems that Amvets players had had with getting paid but didn't mention the problem, because I assumed that Gene would hear from some unpaid customers soon enough. The ten-and-twenty game was still a cash-in, chips-out operation, and all the payment problems had come about in the Scoot (no-limit) game, so the limit game was still fairly lively and full of players. The two thugs who'd been running things in Gene's absence were missing, the only time in recent memory that neither of those two was there.

About midafternoon, I'd tossed in my cards and was sitting out a hand when I happened to glance up toward the door where Gene sat. One of the no-limit players (my memory has faded some in the past thirty years; it might've been Bob Hooks, but then again it could have been a guy named Troy Phillips, a big-time bookmaker who once was married to the stripper Candy Barr) was leaning on the chip-dispensing counter and bending Gene's ear. Gene was frowning; I knew the topic of the conversation. I also knew that Gene wouldn't like what had been going on; like the rest of the game runners, Gene was no angel, but he did appreciate that keeping the customers happy was critical in running a poker game, just as in any other business. The complaining customer left in a few moments and, as I watched, Gene hauled the phone up from under the counter and made a call. He talked for about five minutes, then hung up and approached the ten-and-twenty game.

Gene waited for the hand in play to be over, then, as the next dealer scooped the cards together, stepped in and leaned on the poker table. "You guys listen up. I'm gonna ask you straight out. Is there anybody here who's owed money by this joint?"

No one spoke up. As regulars in the cash-only ten-and-twenty game, these guys had all collected what they'd won without a problem. Every one of them, however, knew someone from the no-limit table who had money coming, some of them a great deal, but, gambler-like, none of the ten-and-twenty players felt that it was their place to say anything.

"Well, if you know somebody who's owed," Gene said, "you tell 'em they'll get their money in the next twenty-four hours. I just now found out what's been going on while I was away. I'm puttin' a stop to it. I got a meeting set up tonight where I'm gonna get to the bottom of it." Gene returned to the chip-seller's desk, the dealer shuffled the cards, and the game went on.

The game broke up just after dark, another big change from when Gene had run the game; the players sometimes had stayed until dawn. The fact was, the thugs who'd been running the game made us nervous, and rightfully so, and none of us smaller players wanted to be inside the club after nightfall. I was the last to cash in. I nodded good-bye to Gene and headed for the exit.

Just before I went through the door into the street, the two thugs came in. One was a guy in his fifties who'd done time in Mississippi, and the other was an incredibly skinny man in his thirties who was known to have done four armed robberies, and who'd stayed in county jail for over a year even though the police hadn't been able to charge him with any crime and eventually had had to let him go. Both men nodded to me. I went outside with goose bumps raising on my spine the size of spider eggs. I had a bad feeling about what was going to happen in the meeting; since this pair had threatened the poker players who'd tried to collect their winnings, there was no reason to think that they'd be any more cooperative just because Gene was back in town. And the half of the poker take that Gene had coming to him was uncollectible as well, that much I was sure of.

I'd made it halfway to my car when Charles Harrelson parked his Cadillac at the curb across the street, got out, and ambled toward the Amvets Club. (It would be a number of years before Charles's conviction for murdering a federal judge, but he'd been a man to fear for a long, long time. He'd already been to prison once on murder-for-hire charges in connection with the death of a grain dealer in Hearne, Texas—he got a short sentence by ratting out the guy who'd hired him—and would be high on any list of usual suspects in any city in the Southwest. He was the most cold-eyed man I've ever laid eyes on.) I averted my gaze and double-timed it to my car.

I sat behind my steering wheel and watched Charles cross the street. He never so much as glanced in my direction. He stepped up on the curb and walked purposefully into the Amvets Club. I would've bet a lot of money that Gene had no idea that a killer had been invited to join the meeting, and I was pretty sure that Gene wouldn't have made the meeting himself if he'd known that Charles Harrelson would be part of the group. I started the engine and headed for home, relieved that I'd made it out of the place and certain that my days as a player in the Amvets ten-and-twenty game were numbered as hell.

No one I know of has ever laid eyes on Gene since that day, and I may very well be the last person, other than whoever made him disappear, to have seen him alive. Since Gene was on the police department's list of small-time crooks, not much real effort was made to find him—or his corpse—and I suspect that his file is now somewhere in the cold-case archives never to be pulled again. And to be honest, for all I know, Gene may suddenly have decided to move out of town and, even as I write this, is frolicking on some island paradise with a bunch of bikini-wearing nymphets. But I seriously doubt it.

The next day, the two thugs were back running the Amvets game. The game itself died on the vine shortly thereafter, because the high players never got paid and the little guys (meaning the ten-and-twenty players) were frightened to death of the place. Within a week, I'd joined a golf club in the Dallas suburb of Grand Prairie where a businessman's poker game went on daily, and where I was to remain a regular player for the next five years.

Things were tough out there. If you were playing poker for profit in those days, winning was the least of your problems. I once saw a man who'd made a big win at no-limit accosted by three killers on his way out of the poker joint, and forced to play heads-up poker against one of them. It was obvious that the killers weren't going to let the man out of the place with his bankroll no matter what, so he took the path of least resistance, pushed all of his money into the pot with no hand at all, and let the killer win. He did make it home alive that night, sort of a moral victory for him.

There were a few humorous incidents, the most famous and funniest of which had to do with old-time gambler Everett Goolsby and a guy named Charley Boyd. Charley Boyd was said to have killed fifteen men in his life, though the actual figure was probably higher. He was only an occasional poker player, though he did hang around a lot of illegal poker games to keep tabs on who was winning on a regular basis so he'd know which players might be carrying a lot of cash. Charley died young, the result of an exercise-yard stabbing while doing a sentence in the Texas Department of Corrections.

Have I got you in stitches yet? Don't worry, it gets even funnier.

When Everett Goolsby was flush with money, he played poker as high as anyone in the world, and he was just the kind of guy whom Charley Boyd would keep tabs on. One night Charley arrived at the high-rollers' game just after Goolsby had gone home for the night and heard through the table-talk grapevine that Goolsby had made a big five-figure win. Charley had to have felt like kicking himself for missing out on the chance to rob the guy. But one thing about Charley, he had a way of looking at today's loss as tomorrow's gain.

The next morning, Charley called Goolsby on the phone. "I know you made a big win," Charley told him, "and you're lucky that I'm too tired to come over and take the money now, so tell you what, I'm gonna sleep til noon. If I find a package on my porch when I wake up, and if that package has ten thousand dollars inside, I'm gonna be satisfied. If it ain't here, well, sorry, Everett, but I'm gonna come lookin' for you."

True to his word, Charley went to bed and got up just after the noon hour. The ten thousand dollars was on his porch in an envelope, thus completing the only known case of anyone committing a robbery over the phone. Yes, it happened, and before you start calling for the butterfly nets to come after Goolsby, consider his options. Charley wasn't kidding and Goolsby knew it, so Goolsby could either surrender the ten thousand dollars peacefully or get ready to defend his property when Charley came after him. Goolsby wasn't a killer, but Charley was, and the end result of defying Charley's instructions could very well have been death for Goolsby. Some might think that Goolsby should've called the police, but that really wasn't an option. To begin with, the cops would have looked askance at Goolsby's story about someone robbing him over the phone. Also, since their complaining witness would've had a lengthy gambling rap sheet as well, the cops' first move likely would have been to jail Goolsby on illegal gambling charges, so instead of ten thousand dollars of Goolsby's bankroll ending up in Charley Boyd's pocket, every dime he owned could easily have ended up in the police evidence locker never to be seen again.

These tales of cheats and robbers pretty much describe the world that this just-out-of-college babe in the woods, wandered into back in the 1960s, wide-eyed and innocent as they came. Hell, I wasn't even a very good poker player at the time (although I thought I was) and had to get very lucky to win in those games even if no one cheated me or stuck a pistol in my face. By all rights I should have been broke in just a few weeks, but an incredible streak of luck—even hotter than the one I experienced after my college freshman year—showed up to save me. I became a major winner within a very short period of time; got very cocky, as all youngsters tend to do when hitting one ball after another out of the park; and very quickly appeared on the cheats' and hijackers' radar screen, not to mention caused more than one poker shark to tear his hair.

As far as my poker education went, I couldn't have been more fortunate, because I learned the poker life in just the opposite order from most people. Nearly all novices trying to learn Hold 'Em are so caught up in the intricacies of the game that they have no time to look back over their shoulders to see who might be trailing them, often with tragic results. In my own case, I was winning from the get-go, so I was convinced that I was such a good player that I needed no improvement (even though my play was absolutely dreadful at the time, a fact that I'd learn the hard way when my cards eventually cooled off), but I did quickly learn the nonplaying pitfalls out there in the poker world and how to avoid them. There were painful lessons; a couple of guys cold decked me out of twenty-five hundred dollars one night in a no-limit game, and gun-toting masked men robbed me on two separate occasions. I was winning enough to overcome such tragedies, but had I not been dumb lucky at the poker table, the cheating incident plus the holdups would have so damaged my finances that I would have had to go back to changing tires.

So now, for your reference in the "poker lifestyle" section of your notebook, I give you my Pigeon's Postulates for Secure Play:

1. **I play poker only in legally licensed casinos, or occasionally in illegal backroom parlors where I know the game runner well enough that I don't have to worry about any set-up hijackings or cheating incidents (and, yes, woefully, there are game runners around who will finger players they know to be flush with cash for a percentage of the hijackers' take, and who aren't above cooperating in an occasional cold decking in return for a piece of the action).**
2. **I carry with me to the game only enough money to play; how much you can afford to risk is better known to you than anyone, but there is no point whatsoever**

in tempting hijackers (or yourself, after you've reached your pre-set limit but are still on tilt) with sums greater than those intended for play.

3. I play in daylight hours whenever possible, coming and going when the sun is high in the sky. Strictly daytime play isn't a requirement in Las Vegas, where security is tight twenty-four/seven, but see my previous comments on Las Vegas play and its profit potential. Every place else that I'm aware of where poker is legal or there's an illegal backroom game where I'm not afraid to go, daylight is my friend. This is especially true in poker parlors and casinos located on Indian reservations. (Indian casinos are nearly all in freestanding buildings with enormous parking lots and interstate highway frontage, and once you exit the casino in the direction of your car, you're on your own. Sections of these parking lots are dimly lit at night, and there are plenty of ideal places for hijackers to lie in wait for you, rob you, take your cell phone as well, and then zoom out onto the interstate while you're still trying to find a pay phone to call the law.) On those rare occasions when I do play after dark, I leave my winnings and all my cash except for walking-around money on deposit with the casino or illegal poker room (where, of course, I know the game runner quite well before i'll even go near the place). It's somewhat inconvenient to have to go back in daylight hours to collect my money, but much preferable to having some creep make off with my bankroll.

And as for you, if you are seriously considering poker as a form of secondary (or primary) income, and if you live within easy driving distance of a legal casino poker room (with the exception of the precautions necessary at Indian casinos or any casino located in a rural area near an interstate), then you should have little to worry about regarding security. There are, however, a number of major American cities where card rooms are still illegal—New York City and Miami come immediately to mind, followed closely by Dallas and Houston—and where a professional can ply his trade only in speakeasy-type poker joints. It's possible to earn a living in those places (even though their very nature—which eliminates the drop-in business found at legal casino games—attracts a lot of really good players, so the games are generally tougher than what you'll find in a casino), but before embarking on a steady diet of illegal poker rooms, I'd study the precautions given in this chapter very carefully. The dangers encountered in frequenting illegal poker parlors as I've outlined have been, are, and will be existent forever, and anyone trying to negotiate those back-street waters need be constantly on his or her guard.

7

Out West

Or,
I Go to Las Vegas and Lose My Way Home

It took a minute or two after the shotgun blast split the silence, but the odor of burnt gunpowder drifted into the bedroom and up my nostrils. All of the zip-cuffed men seemed dazed, though a few sets of eyes moved rapidly from side to side in the players' heads as if the captives were searching in vain for an exit. I sat on the edge of the bed and didn't move. My thoughts were sluggish, my senses dulled. Christ, had the hijackers killed someone? And with one already shot, was there any reason for Monkey One and Monkey Two not to waste the rest of us to eliminate witnesses?

Heavy footfalls sounded in the hallway and then Monkey One came into the room, the shotgun cradled in the crook of his arm. Wisps of smoke rose from the double barrels. The squatty thug came over and stood over me. He waved the shotgun first in my direction, then at the hallway door. "You," he said, "come with me."

Very few people who've taken up poker as a profession can resist the urge to try moving to Las Vegas, though most end up slinking home with their tail between their legs. No joke, Las

Vegas is an extremely tough spot in which to make it, and the card room at the Bellagio is to poker aspirants what New York City and Hollywood are to acting hopefuls—where all the stars who never were are parkin' cars and pumpin' gas. But there are a few who do quite well, and the successful Las Vegas pros whom I know have one thing in common: they never tried Las Vegas until they were ready. The sad but true usual tale has the cocky youngster on an incredibly lucky winning streak deciding that he's going to take Nevada in the same manner as he's taken the boys back home, breezing into town with a pocket full of cash and, if he's lucky, ending up with barely enough for a bus ticket home. I moved to Las Vegas only after I'd been a poker player for several years, and though I was lucky enough to leave town with quite a bit more money than I came in with, I firmly believe that I owe my success to keeping my head on straight and the blinders on. In this chapter, I'll try to explain what I'm talking about.

It took time, but I finally reached a level where, even when I look back from today's vantage point, I was a pretty good Hold 'Em player. Naturally, at the time I thought I was a poker shark at *every* stage of my development, but I'm talking about reaching a level where I had the respect of even the pros, and where in games against all manner of competition I'd come out ahead if the cards would break even for me. I'd built a fairly hefty bankroll that wasn't in danger of disappearing during the monthslong losing streaks that happen to all of us, and before I ever considered trying Las Vegas out, I'd reached a personal goal of having enough put aside so that I could live for a year without winning a dime. Very few so-called professionals achieve the financial shape in which I found myself; most spend money as fast as they make it, and when the inevitable losing streak hits, they have nothing in reserve to see their way through (the frugality-versus-the-free-spending aspect of the poker player is no different from what you'll find in all forms of making a living; everywhere you turn there are those people who hang on to their money and those who piss it away, and that's the way things are and always have been).

From a playing standpoint I could calculate the odds of making any draw with lightning speed. During the deal, as I barely glanced at my pocket cards, I knew instinctively what cards to play relative to my position and which ones to throw away (and in that regard I'd reached the independent thinking stage where if I disagreed with Sklansky and certain other gurus I'd go with my own decisions rather than sticking to theirs). There was no situation that came about during play where I felt any uncertainty over what to do, and in nearly every instance my decisions were the correct ones. You could draw out on me and even occasionally beat me with the best hand going in, but you couldn't outthink me and you could never accuse me of making stupid plays.

And, oh, yeah, I could recognize the nuts at every juncture during a hand.

Everyone except the really expert Hold 'Em players will get a big laugh out of that last statement. *Recognize the nuts? Who cares about the nuts? We already know about the nuts, but we wanna know how to pick up tells and shit. How dumb does this guy think we are?*

Pretty dumb, actually, if you don't understand the importance of what I've just said. So here it comes, readers, in postulate form: **The most important skill in limit Hold 'Em once the flop appears is the ability to know the nuts on the flop, on the turn, and on the river, and the ability to know what cards can change the nuts and what cards will have no effect on the nuts as the hand progresses.**

Why? Because unless you know the best possible two-card

hand based on what's on the board at all times, and the probable draws your opponents might hold, it will be impossible to evaluate your own hand as it relates to what you're up against.

What say? Okay, rather than repeat myself *ad nauseum*, I'll try teaching by example.

In a ten-handed game you pick up A♥A♣ on the button. By the time the betting gets around to you, there are two players who've called the blinds and the player to your immediate right has raised. What you read into the raise depends on the player. If the raiser is a weak player, he could have a big hand or he could have something like KQ, which looks like a big hand to a novice but which we know to be one of the worst hands he could have in this situation. If he's a pretty good player, he could have a marginal hand like 89 suited, and merely be trying to steal the button from you. Regardless of what the raiser's holding, he's given you the golden opportunity to double raise with your pocket rockets and eliminate some competition; your double raise knocks out both blind players, the two players who called the blind come back in for the double raise, and the guy to your right calls as well, so going into the flop you're up against three players. You're now ready for the flop, and you must be aware of the following before the flop hits the table: **In a four-handed game, AA is a slight underdog to the field, though it's a huge favorite head-up against any individual hand, and whether you're going to win or lose money in this situation over the total number of times that it will occur during a hundred years of steady play depends entirely on the strength of your play after the flop, and the strength of your play after the flop in turn depends entirely on your ability to react to the cards that hit the board.**

And after you repeat *that* mouthful in your head a couple of times, the flop comes J♠,9♠,10♦.

Though you shouldn't panic, you should be aware that you have just gotten about the worst flop possible to A♥A♣. Though KQ is, going in, one of the worst hands that a player can have before the flop in this situation, the flop has now made KQ the nuts, and the weaker the players who've called your double raise, the greater the likelihood that one of them has KQ. Conversely, if three near-expert players have seen the flop, the chances that one of them has KQ are practically nonexistent, and you can pretty well eliminate that hand from the list of possibilities. In the worst-case scenario (where a novice holds KQ against you), you do have the saving grace that if the player is bad enough to stand a double pre-flop raise with that piece-of-crap hand, he's probably also bad enough to pull the Weak Player's Fourth-Street Check-Raise (see *Play Poker Like a Pigeon*, my previous book, for a full explanation of this bonehead maneuver) from his bag of tricks, and though he'll check and merely call your mandatory post-flop bet, when he tries to check-raise you on Fourth Street you can get away from the hand and save a bundle. Even if no one has KQ and you're still ahead in the hand, with three players opposing you, one or more will nearly always have one queen, giving those players an open-end straight draw, and someone else will likely have two pocket spades to give him a flush draw. Also, there's the always present probability that someone will hold a jack and will have flopped top pair with a pretty good kicker (QJ, of course, makes top pair *and* an open-end straight draw), which increases the number of cards that can fall off the deck to beat you by five (three cards that make two pair out of one pair, and two cards that make a pair into trips). At this point you can resign yourself that unless the turn and river produce two cards lower than 6 of which neither is a spade, you're probably going to lose, and you should now turn your thoughts to damage control—figure out when you should fold if the worst comes to pass, in other words. With two aces it's very difficult to admit defeat, but the best players learn to do so or prepare to hock their watches for a bus ticket home.

Of utmost importance is the ability not only to recognize the nuts after the flop in this situation, but also to create a mental list of cards that will almost surely beat you, and get ready to run for cover if one of the cards on your list hits the board. Tight, aggressive play is a must in Hold 'Em, but *stupidly* aggressive play merely because you have two aces is certain suicide.

Now let's switch from worst-case scenario to best case. Same situation, same action before the flop. The three cards that hit the board are J♠,6♥,2♦.

There is no better flop to two aces than the one you're looking at. The pocket cards that have you beat at the moment are JJ, 66, 22, J6, J2, and 62. Absolutely no one, not even the worst player imaginable, would be in the pot with any of the last three combinations (excluding, of course, drunks on tilt, who would come in there no matter what they had in their hands), and no really good player would have seen the flop with only four-way action if he or she held any of the three listed pairs other than jacks (the true odds of flopping a set are about one in seven, but not many players are skillful enough at computing probabilities to know those odds, so you must consider sets of sixes or deuces as possibilities). With two jacks, a good player would re-raise after your button raise before the flop, after which you'd cap the betting (pokerese for making the last permitted raise), so you'd likely be up against two less players than you are, so it's highly unlikely that anyone has a set of jacks. There are no possible straight draws (other than inconceivable ones such as 34, 45, or 35, all of which would be inside draws and not worth a moment's consideration) and no possible flush draws. If it's possible to be freewheeling with two aces, that's what you're doing at the moment. If some really weak player check-raises you on

Fourth Street, then you are surely beaten and should toss your aces then and there, but barring such a calamity the only worry you'll have is a card coming at the end that pairs the board— and it's most likely that only a jack on Fifth Street will actually beat you, since no one with half a brain would stay to the end if all he or she had on the flop was sixes or deuces. Someone might pair his or her kicker, of course, and make two pair to beat you, but you'd have no way of knowing if the player had and would just have to take your medicine and donate to the player. If you should lose this pot you'd have every right to rip your aces in half and bang your head against the wall, but you're too skillful and well grounded as a player to show your ass by doing so.

There are as many situations that can come up in limit Hold 'Em as there are seven-card combinations in a deck (millions; I won't bore you with computing the exact figure), but the point I'm trying to get across here is this: *I wasn't worth a flip as a Hold 'Em player until I learned to make quick calculations in my head, not only regarding the odds of my own hand improving, but also regarding the best possible two-card hand in relation to the board at all times (which, depending on how strongly my opponents played their hands in relation to how well I knew them, gave me a pretty good idea of what they had) and what cards yet to come would or would not help other players, and what cards would or would not help my own hand.* So while the novice's belief that anyone ought to be able to figure out the nuts by looking at the board is true, the really necessary calculations of the various possibilities regarding cards yet to come are outside the novice's realm of understanding and will remain so until the novice has played many, many hours of Hold 'Em over a number of years.

I once played a hand that drew a lot of *oohs* and *ahs* from other poker players, and though many seem to think that my actions in the hand were a stroke of genius, I consider what I did mere business as usual based on my calculation of the nuts and the possibilities of what could happen on the turn and on the river. The *circumstance* of the hand was one in a zillion, but I still maintain that there was nothing remarkable about what I did. The date was June 9, 1983; the place was a country club in Grand Prairie, Texas; and the hand was played sometime between eight and eight-thirty in the evening. The date and place and time stand out in my mind not because of my own brilliant play, but because of the near-impossible way that the cards came out in this one particular hand.

It was my deal. I looked down after putting out two-card hands to one and all and found two sixes in the pocket. This particular golf club game was notorious as the place where all the pros in the area were chomping at the bit to play, and I'll admit that it was the softest spot with the worst group of players going at it consistently that I've ever found. The game stayed ten handed every day from around noon until the wee hours; there were two or three competent players at the club (even one pro other than me, as a matter of fact), while the rest hadn't a clue and seemed in no hurry to find one. I don't say this to knock the players personally, merely to note that the overall poor quality of play in the game had a lot to do with my eventual decision over what to do in the hand.

Two players had called the blind, as I recall, before the guy to my immediate right raised before the flop. The raiser was a woefully weak player, so I didn't give him credit for being smart enough to try to steal the button; the guy didn't know position from the hole in his ass, so I knew that position didn't dictate his raise and that he had at a minimum two high cards. If he wasn't paired, my sixes had him beat, so I grabbed my golden opportunity and double raised in the hope that everyone else would fold and I could isolate my sixes against the original raiser's AK, AQ, or whatever, my sixes being a slight head-up favorite over any unpaired hand. The small blind did fold, but the man in the big-blind position came over the top and called the double raise; I didn't attribute any meaning to the big blind's call, because most of the players in this game subscribed to the "in for a penny, in for a pound" theory in regard to the blinds and once their forces were in the pot were by God going to see the flop no matter what. Everyone else except the original raiser tossed in his hand. The original raiser popped me again.

Now I blinked. While I don't believe that ego has any place at the poker table, I do think it's just as important for a good player to know how he's regarded by others as it is for him to be familiar with the way that others in the game play their hands. I'd beaten the country club game regularly for a couple of years at the time, and while the other players stuck to their own form of racehorse when knocking heads among themselves, they tended to react differently to bets from me and a couple of other competent players. They generally gave my hands a lot of respect—*too much* respect, as a matter of fact, which had enabled me to run a few successful bluffs that I never would have attempted in a limit game against stiff competition—and the original raiser in the pot never would have repopped me unless he had really strong pocket cards. I immediately put him on a big pair, jacks or higher (as it turned out I was giving him just a little bit too much credit), so I only called his re-raise and made up my mind that unless the flop made me a set of sixes, I'd toss in my hand at the first post-flop action.

The flop came 9♠,6♦,2♥.

I'll make one more quick point here, having to do with my contempt for the Weak Player's Fourth-Street Check-Raise and why I keep harping on the fact that it's the worst play in Hold 'Em. After all that pre-flop action, most novices would have played their set of sixes very cozily, called with wide-eyed innocence all post-flop bets, then let the hammer down on the turn when the betting limit doubled, and to have played this hand in that manner would have cost me a bundle. Aggressive play is imperative if you are to be a successful Hold 'Em player, and all good post-flop hands should be played in the same manner so that when you bet or raise after the flop your opponents don't know whether to put you on top pair and a good kicker or some really monster hand such as the one I had.

The guy in big-blind position checked—which didn't surprise me at all, because this guy, under the "in for a penny, in for a pound" theory, would have seen the flop no matter what—and the player to my right, the original pre-flop raiser, fired a bet my way. I raised without hesitation and immediately saw confusion on the bettor's face: Had I flopped a monster, or was I just testing his hand? I waited for the big-blind man to toss in his cards, after which the original raiser and I would have a go at it.

The big-blind man called the original bet, my raise, and added a raise of his own.

To say that I was stunned wouldn't tell the half of it; suddenly, the man in the big-blind position had gone from no hand at all to the near nuts in the wink of an eye. He was a weak player who had obviously flopped Gargantua; who had checked in preparation for using the old Fourth-Street Check-Raise maneuver; and who, upon seeing that his opponents apparently had big hands as well, had decided not to wait to let the hammer down. It was at that point that it occurred to me that my set of sixes might not be the best hand after all.

And just as *that* thought pushed its way into my consciousness, the player on my right called my raise, the big-blind man's raise, and added his own raise.

It was now my turn to act. There are four raises permitted in limit Hold 'Em, so I could raise if I decided to do so. I studied the board: 9♠, 6♦, 2♥. No possible straight, no possible flush. A pocket hand of 78 would give a player an open-ended straight draw, but there wasn't the remotest possibility that either of two weak players, each raising the maximum possible, was on any kind of draw, especially with a player they both feared—me—up against them. When the original bettor had acted, since he was also the pre-flop driver in this pot, he could have held an overpair (tens or higher) at the very minimum, but when I'd raised and the big-blind man had raised as well, and then the original bettor had kept on firing, any possibility that he had only an overpair had gone out the window. The big-blind man could've flopped two pair, but it was more likely that he'd flopped a set just as I had. In my long, long life at the poker table, I'd never seen three players flop sets in the same hand, but it now occurred to me that that might have been exactly what had happened. I had no doubt that one of these dudes had flopped a set of nines.

I then did something that I had never done before, nor have I since. The player sitting beside me, who'd folded before the flop, was a guy named Junior Hess. Junior, a guy well known around the poker world and a very close friend of mine, was the only other pro in the game. I announced to the table at large that I was folding, then tossed my pocket cards, facedown, over to Junior. "Here," I said, "you would've played these." (There was nothing out of line in my action here; it's fine to show another player your hole cards as long as when the cards are all out your folded hand gets turned faceup so that the entire table can have a look.) Junior glanced at my cards, maintained a blank expression just as I'd known he would, and gave me a brief nod.

As the hand played out, both players raised the maximum after every card and—assuming we were playing ten and twenty, though the game could've been twenty and forty or even higher since we played all kinds of limits as the nights wore on and the losers wanted to play higher—had I stayed in I would've shoveled a couple hundred bucks more into the pot than I already had. On the end, the big-blind man showed pocket deuces, the original raiser showed pocket nines, and the big-blind man threw a fit and tore his pocket cards in half. Junior Hess showed my pocket cards, as he was required to do, and I heard a lot of gee whizzes and how'd you do thats for the rest of that night and for months to come. No one I knew had ever witnessed three flopped sets in one hand, and no one seemed to be able to believe that I'd folded. In the past year, I've run into people who were in the game, who've brought up the hand in conversations with me, and since the hand was played twenty-five years ago, I guess it's stuck in some people's memories.

And here's why there was nothing remarkable about my play that night: I recognized the nuts at the outset and also knew what cards could come off the deck to change the nuts as the hand played itself out, and what the chances were that any of those cards could help me. No two pocket cards would have gone with the 9,6,2 flop in three different suits to form a made straight or flush; otherwise, I would've been in to the bitter end in hopes that the board would pair (a set will become either a full house or quads by the time the river card appears just about a third of the time, and the two-way action I was getting would've made it worthwhile to stay in if I'd thought a full house would win). Against a couple of really strong players I might've stayed as well (or at least I would've taken the last raise after the flop and hung around until Fourth Street, when the two other players probably would've convinced me once and for all that at least one of them had me beat), because good players might very well test the post-flop waters with raises if they hold something like 78 suited—representing strength after the flop to slow down the action and possibly get a cheaper, or even free, draw on Fourth Street—or even A9 suited, though it's highly unlikely that A9 would have lured an expert into the pot to begin with. Up against two novices, however, there was no chance that either had enough finesse to play the flop really strong on a draw, or even with top pair to go with an ace kicker, and up against me— whom both of them feared—they wouldn't have let the hammer down with as little as two pair either. And once I'd made up my mind that both players probably had sets and that one of them had two nines in the pocket, it was easy to calculate that the only card that could fall off the deck to save me on the turn or river was the case six. The odds of catching the case six were 2 in 43, and I would've gotten only two for one on my money if I'd been lucky enough to win. So I folded.

While this is an extreme example, it does stress my point. At the time I made the play in question I'd been on the poker circuit, off and on, for twenty years or so, and I'm dead certain that I wouldn't have had the know-how to do what I did until I'd been around for at least ten of those years. To survive against strong competition in limit Hold 'Em, you must have a feel for where you stand in every hand at all times; even the best are wrong every once in a while, but in the long run the player making the fewest mistakes is the one who will come out on top.

Years ago I played quite a bit of no-limit poker as well, and before I launch into any discussion of no-limit strategy, I want to point something out. Not only does limit Hold 'Em require more skill than the shove-it-all-in variety seen prominently today on ESPN, but limit poker is, for the most part, a much bigger game with more money on the line.

And, yeah, that's what I said. First of all, you have to blot the World Series of Poker and all televised tournaments out of your mind, because those are set-up, made-for-prime-time events and we're talking about the real world of poker here. You've also got to forget the highrollers' room at the Bellagio—which is, after all, one little fifty-by-thirty space and the only spot on the planet where fools bet sky-high and bigger fools call—and concentrate on the other 99 percent of the poker games, legal and otherwise, that go on every day in different parts of America and the world at large.

In the average casino poker room, you'll find limit games ranging from $4 and $8 limit up to $30 and $60 limit, with several levels in between. Most experienced players feel that someone should have twenty times the maximum limit—in other words, $160 in the $4 and $8, and $1,200 in the $30 and $60—as a buy-in in order to participate in enough hands to have a legitimate shot at winning. Those are really bare minimum figures, and losing players will often buy in two or three times as their stacks diminish, so $400 losses are common in $4 and $8, and $3,000–$5,000 losses at $30 and $60 are not unusual.

So let's compare these figures with the standard no-limit game. Not all poker rooms even offer no-limit play, and those that do stick generally to $1 and $2 or $2 and $5 blinds. The effect of the size of the blinds on the amount of money changing hands in the game is pretty well lost on the novice—inexperienced players believe that no-limit is no-limit and what the hell—so just think about the blind structure for a moment. While Texas Hold 'Em might owe its current popularity to television exposure, the lure that attracts the millions of new players to the no-limit games is the same something for nothing philosophy that attracts the ghetto dwellers to the lottery. When playing no-limit with $1 and $2 forced bets, you can see a lot of cards and flops for a $25 buy-in, and $100 will set you up nicely in games with $2 and $5 blinds. Every year, some mope who began with a $25 buy-in to an Internet tourney makes it to the final table at the WSOP and walks off with a few million, and though such well-publicized strokes of fortune have thousands upon thousands of novices chomping at the bit to saddle up and say stone faced, "All in," with cameras grinding in the background, the end result of this nonsense is that the house offering the tournament cleans up on the rake, sending one player home happy with the rest of the players having nothing to show for their trouble. An example: While doing research for this book, I came across one Internet tourney offering a $10,000 seat at the WSOP as its one and only prize that signed up 15,000 entrants who ponied up five-buck entry fees. *The tourney organizers profited $65,000 and the tournament was over in less than an hour.* Does this sound a bit like the lottery? If it doesn't, then I'm not getting my point across; due to its risk-a-little-to-win-a-lot format, no-limit poker is assuming its place in the casino world right alongside the Big Wheel and the slot machine. And though I'll get backlash from this statement, I continue to believe that no-limit tourney entrants exhibit no more skill than the hundreds upon hundreds of grandmotherly types who park their fannies in hard-seated chairs for hours while they poke buttons on the slots and blink at the flashing lights until they're bleary-eyed.

I'll stick a little anecdote in here to demonstrate. I have two twenty-something nephews by marriage, and since my poker-playing exploits are legendary—among my own family, at any rate—the last time I saw these two youngsters they couldn't wait to tell me that they'd started their own Wednesday night Hold 'Em game. "Great," I said. "I'll bet you guys are enjoying that. What limits are you playing?"

The biggest kid, a barrel-chested towhead, drew up to his full height and announced rather testily, "We don't got no stinkin' limits. We are all no-limit guys."

Jesus Christ, I thought. "Well, I don't know if I could afford to play in that," I said.

"Well," the kid said, looking sort of sheepish, "buy-in's five bucks." He tightened his jaw. "But the first chance we get, we shove it all in," he said.

Just a few months after this encounter, the same kid won a seat in the WSOP playing on the Internet. He didn't last past the first day's action, but he was there with bells on.

But that ain't gonna be you, is it? You're going to be a *poker player*.

So now, once and for all, and in supercondensed form, here is the part of the book that a lot of readers have been waiting for: The Poker Pigeon's Ultimate Guide to No-Limit Play. I had thought about asking the publisher to perforate the next few pages so that you would easily tear them out like checks or credit card payment coupons and take them along with you to the next big game, but I figured the expense involved in doing so would raise the price of the book to the point that you might not be so eager to buy it.

Actually the risk-a-little, win-a-lot lure existed in no-limit poker forty years ago, but the way it worked in illegal house games was quite different from today's tournament-crazy world, where every player must start with the same amount of chips. My first exposure to Scoot (and you'll have to excuse me if I keep calling no-limit poker by its archaic moniker, in the same way that some really old golfers refer to certain clubs as mashies and niblicks and whatnot) came on Dallas's Lower Greenville Avenue at the Amvets Club, where I played off and on from the mid-1960s to the early 1980s, and where the game featured blinds of $10 and $25, not to mention daily play from some of the most famous poker stars in the world. The minimum buy-in was $250, and although I was never sure exactly which superstar dreamed up the forced-bet structure, the guy who did was brilliant; the game was set up so that the pros triumphed nearly every day and it was virtually impossible for the sucker to win.

And here's why. Big-name Scoot players of the past ruled by intimidation and fear, just as they do today, only forty years ago they were more brazen about it. They'd shill up to the no-limit table with a couple thousand dollars in chips apiece and spend their time with folded hands, shooting the bull, until the first live one showed up and the game could begin for real. The outsiders who dropped in were just like today's tournament players, intent on risking a little for a shot at a bonanza, but the blind structure ensured that the $250 minimum buy-in didn't take the sucker very far. Every time the deal went around the table, every player had to put up $35 in forces, so the guy with only $250 in front of him couldn't afford to wait for a primo hand because in a very short while he'd ante his bankroll away. Today analytical guests on ESPN say that not only can the high-dollar pros read other players like a book, but they have no regard whatsoever for the dollar and consider money a mere tool of the trade. That sort of statement sounds good on television, but when it came to the old-time high players, that statement wasn't quite true. For a fact they did think nothing of shoving thousands into the pot on a cold bluff, but there was a calculated method to this madness, because they knew that except on the rare occasions when the $250 players had flopped the nuts or near nuts, or picked up pocket aces, the lesserweights couldn't afford to call.

And in case you don't appreciate the pressure that the suckers were under in this situation, picture yourself as a player trying to turn $250 into thousands sitting down in a cash game among self-assured men whom you've heard of all your poker-playing life and then having one of those guys shove an all-in bet your way with you holding, say, top pair with an ace kicker after the flop. The bettor has a stack in front of him that the $250 hardly dents, but if you should call and lose, you're out of the game. Regardless of what decision you make regarding calling or folding, your spit is going to dry up and your heart will try to pound its way through your breastbone. Probably you'll have the best hand at the moment, but what if you don't?

And even if you should call and win the pot, the bettor can put you all in two or three more times before you have a stack anywhere near equal to his, not to mention that each of his buddies has a pile of chips as big or bigger. For you to win in this game you're going to have to go all in four or five times and win every one of those pots, and the odds against you achieving such a streak are astronomical. In truth, you'd be better off bucking casino odds at craps or blackjack. The outsider was simply outmonied in those games, and in no-limit poker that's like saying the novices had zero chance to win. (Whether they were outmonied on a cash basis is suspect; I told in an earlier chapter about my first dumb-lucky experience with no-limit poker where, forty years later, I'm still waiting for my money, but as a newcomer to the game who's been required to pony up cash for the chips in front of you, you don't know that the poker heroes in the game are all on credit, and you assume that the buy-in rules are the same for everybody. And since the sucker almost never won in those games, whether or not he could've collected had he come out on top was, in the long run, irrelevant.)

There was only one sucker I ever saw who didn't perform according to the plan and donate to the hustlers' cause, 250 bucks at a time, and that particular citizen wasn't rated a sucker once he'd played a few times. His name was Ken Smith, a bearded roly-poly man who weighed close to four hundred pounds, and who'd inherited a successful family contracting business that kept him in near-unlimited funds. Not only could Smitty match the hustlers stack for stack and then some; he could bring cash and always get more, which made the pros' mouths water until they got a load of Smitty's style of play. To begin with, he didn't know poker from Pokemon, but he was no stranger to gambling propositions (he'd once backed a Las Vegas blackjack counter for big bucks and stayed with the proposition until several hundred thousand dollars in losses convinced him that the card-counting system didn't work and never was going to); he was a world-class tournament chess player; and, worst of all for the hustlers, he understood money and how to use it against his opponents. The first time he played in the no-limit game, Smitty brought the usual $250 buy-in, but after he saw what the game was all about, he showed up the following afternoon with $10,000 in his pocket. And though he barely knew how to put two cards with five to create a poker hand when starting out, he was highly intelligent and a fast learner, and within a couple of weeks after beginning to play at the no-limit table, he had the game pretty well decimated and the hustlers in fast retreat. Within a couple of years he was to reach the final table at the WSOP at the Horseshoe, though his playing skills were no better then than the first time he sat in at the Amvets. I've seen most of 'em close up in my time—Bob Hooks, Bill Smith, Stu Ungar, Bobby Baldwin, etc., etc., etc.—but I learned more about no-limit poker by watching Ken Smith operate for six months than I did from years of observing those other guys. Like many grossly obese people, Smitty died young of a heart attack, and that's a dirty shame.

Smitty was apt to come into a no-limit pot with any two cards (much like Brunson, only with Smitty the propensity to start out weak was even stronger), and unless his opponent held a monstrous hand and was trying to trap him, it was a mistake to check to Smitty, because no matter what he had he'd come firing. His first move on arriving at a game in the afternoon was to check out the chip stacks in front of everyone at the table, and the moment he sat down he'd have twice as much in front of him as the next biggest pile. The hustlers were used to putting the sucker's 250 bucks all in on a regular basis, but when it came to Smitty, the shoe was on the other foot, and how. One afternoon I saw him make an all-in move and then, while his opponent considered a call, turned one of his pocket cards faceup.

The card was a three, and since the opponent had two face cards in his hand he was forced to call. Smitty lost that particular pot, but not before his opponent nearly had a heart attack as the turn and river cards hit the board while Smitty sat there grinning as if nothing could ever bother him. In retrospect, I wonder why the hustlers never changed the game to limit poker in order to restrict Smitty's money advantage (which was the strategy that Brunson and a gang of pros used to beat a bottomless-pocketed Dallas banker named Andy Beal in the biggest poker game ever played), and I believe to this day that in an ultra-high-limit game, Smitty would have been easy pickings for those guys.

In addition to the piles of money he brought to the table, Smitty had just the type of abrasive personality (which could have been an act, I suppose; I was never really sure that his nastiness was for real) that goaded the hustlers over the line in trying to beat him, shooting their games all to hell and putting some of the best players in the world so far on tilt that they never recovered, and causing me, years later, to create the Poker Pigeon's Ken Smith–Inspired Winning Strategy for No-Limit Poker: Basically, if you are able to bring such an unlimited supply of cash to the table that at all times you can break any other player in the game, then no-limit poker is the game for you, and you won't need to worry about playing skills, because you're not going to need any; you need merely keep putting your opponents all in until you win a hand.

If you are, however, mortal, like the rest of us, and are likewise without the U.S. Mint as a financial backer, then if you want to have any chance at all of winning in a cash no-limit game you must develop certain basic playing strategies. And notice that I said *any* chance of winning, and that nowhere will I call my no-limit playing hints any sort of winning strategy, because in no-limit poker I don't believe such a thing exists. There are ways of playing that are better than others, of course, just as there are blackjack strategies that will limit your losses, but I believe if you continue in no-limit cash games for long enough, one dumb-lucky draw out from a well-heeled sucker will eventually send you home in your underwear. Thus it has been with every no-limit guru I've ever known, and thus I believe it will always be. (Keep in mind while reading the following that there is no connection between cash-game play and tournament play; tournaments like the WSOP require entirely different playing strategies, and as long as you understand the odds against your winning and can afford to lose the buy-in, I suppose you can enter whatever tournaments you choose. You should remember, though, that in tournament play, prudent cash-game strategy pretty much goes out the window.)

So now the teacher will teach without conviction, which makes my advice suspect to begin with, but let me tell you up front that my no-limit strategy is compiled from pros who are supposed to know what they're talking about. Basically, good no-limit players come in three categories: (1) Big Chip Stackers with unlimited access to funds (as we've just discussed), who bring so much money to the table that their playing skills become next to irrelevant; (2) conservative players who throw away all but the primo starting hands and try to knock out inferior hands before the flop so as to give their own hands a better chance of winning; and (3) Wild Man Willy types who come into pots with just about any two cards, because they know that the payoff for the rare occasions when their inferior pocket cards connect with what's on the board to make winners out of losers is so much greater in no-limit than in limit games. I've already taken a swing at the Big Chip Stackers, so now I'll take dead aim at the other two categories.

The Conservatives. We're talking about the tightasses (and you thought we were finished with them when we left college poker, didn't you?), who have a better chance in no-limit Hold 'Em than in a limit game, but who end up on the short end of the stick in the long run, just as they do at the limit tables. At first glance, the strategy of sitting back and waiting for something like AK and then putting in a substantial raise in order to eliminate the suited connectors, small pairs, and such before the flop seems like sound play, but in no-limit poker this method is even more flawed than in a limit game. This strategy's success depends too heavily on other players' weaknesses, mainly their inability to fold KQ, KJ, K10, and the like, and thus come into pots where they start out seriously behind. The tightass ploy works better in casino games with, say, one- and two-dollar blinds, because those are the cheap games where you can see a lot of pocket cards for very little money; where the beginners play; and where, therefore, you are likely to find more suckers ready to challenge your AK with inferior hands containing a couple of face cards. Good players recognize the tightass very quickly and won't challenge him or her in a pot without really primo cards of their own (and I'm talking about big pairs, or AK at a minimum) or smaller pocket cards that are suited connectors, hands that, should they match up well with the board, will likely take the tightass's bankroll in one fell swoop. Tightasses in no-limit Hold 'Em make small to moderate wins regularly and lose small amounts in sessions where the really strong hands don't ever come to them, but when they hit a streak where their primo pocket cards get beat a few times, the tightass's losses are staggering. A tightass cannot win in Hold 'Em in the long run, limit or no-limit, and I'll probably be repeating that phrase on my deathbed.

The Wild Man Willy types. Old-time high players will tell you that once upon a time the most feared man alive in a no-limit game was a Texan named Everett Goolsby, and considering that Goolsby's contemporaries included both Brunson and Moss, that's saying a mouthful. Goolsby wasn't the best but he was the most unpredictable; he was apt to play in raised pots with just about any two-card combination imaginable, and Goolsby was capable of decimating any game in record time. The closest resemblance to Goolsby-type play that you'll see on modern television is the Swede Gus Hansen, but you must remember that while Hansen plays in tournaments where his losses are limited to his buy-ins, Goolsby injected his own brand of madness into cash games where every player's ass was on the line. Since any sort of flop might hit Goolsby right in the breadbasket, and since he'd bluff with the same panache as when he had the nuts, when Goolsby would start betting after the flop, the other players in the game didn't have the slightest idea what to do. When Goolsby was a bit short of funds—as he was about half the time—if good players could hang with him and match him bet for bet for long enough, they'd end up winning what was left of his bankroll, but when Goolsby was flush with enough cash to put the largest stack in the game in front of him, he was nigh unbeatable. His wanton style of play was a lot like Ken Smith's, and though Goolsby lacked Smitty's inherited wealth, he was a much better player than Smitty and therefore a lot more dangerous. And though I believe that in no-limit play the Wild Man Willy strategy is ultimately just as suicidal as it is in a limit game, in no-limit poker it is much more apt to break the bank.

Most newcomers to no-limit poker will take the conservative road, because even if the novice is well heeled, he'll be afraid to put so much cash on the line at the outset, and taking up the Wild Man Willy style requires the same sort of experience as expressed in *Play Poker Like a Pigeon (and Take the Money Home)*, because before anyone can successfully play in an unpredictable fashion, he or she must know the rules of good *predictable* play in order to understand just what sort of strategy he or she is deviating from. Of the three types of no-limit player, I personally rate the Wild Man Willy as second behind the Big Chip Stacker as the most likely to win in any given game, with the conservative bringing up the rear by a mile or so. But having said that, I will now, once and for all, explain in detail my belief that in cash no-limit play absolutely no one will come out ahead in the long run.

The problem is in the limit itself or, more specifically, the lack of one. Let's compare a good no-limit Hold 'Em player to a house dealer putting out blackjack hands, with the dealer having the normal mathematical advantage over the players, only where the house lets the players remove the limit and bet whatever they want to. No matter how many hands the dealer wins, if the players' pockets are deep enough, they can merely double their bets after each hand. The first hand that they win—and no matter how bad their play they will eventually have to win one—will put them ahead of the game, and every hand they win thereafter will put them even farther ahead. Where there is no betting limit, the skillful player loses his or her mathematical advantage, and the foregoing is just as true in poker as it is in any casino game. Let's examine the three categories of no-limit Hold 'Em player that I've described and see what result each can expect in the long run.

As I said before, the Big Chip Stackers have the biggest advantage, just as the house with its deep pockets has the edge over the individual players in blackjack even if the players are allowed to bet without limits, but where the limit is lifted the player eventually can double up after losing hands until one win on her part will be enough to turn the house from a comfortable winner into a serious loser. In a Hold 'Em game where one player has five thousand dollars in front of her and another has only five hundred, the short-stacked player need only win four hands in a row to break the Big Chip Stacker, and even if the Big Chip Stacker is one of those players who can keep bringing more piles to the table, after about ten wins in a row by the Short Stacker, the Big Chip Stacker will be seriously hurt no matter how deep her pockets happen to be. Some may be reading this and thinking, *Ten in a row? Impossible!* But it's far from impossible, and ten-streaks in blackjack or head-up poker happen every day.

The tightass player would last the shortest period of time without a limit. His primo starting hands, while they'd generally hold a slight edge over the opposition before the flop, would only have to lose once before Mr. Tightass would be out of the game. Wild Willy will have the best chance of winning, *because of* the lack of a limit, but if he keeps playing for long enough, pushing his entire pile into the center of the table time after time on marginal hands, eventually the percentages will catch up with him and he'll go home a loser as well.

So that there will be no mistake as to what I'm saying, let it be known that I believe every single cash-game no-limit poker player is destined to lose in the long run. And, yes, I've seen superstar interviews on ESPN where the poker pro sits beside the pool at his multimillion-dollar home, but keep in mind that the Big-Time Poker Guy might've won the price of the house in a single sitting and bought the fancy pad for cash, and that within a few months he might have to sell the house to scare up a bankroll and move to a cheap motel. There are other possibilities, of course; often, in the isolated cases of a few prudent poker players, they will buy their home with money earned exclusive of poker winnings. Brunson, for example, has been in on more than one big-money sports-betting operation, has made land and apartment house investments, and is currently the host of the online poker operation at doylesroom.com, a position that pays a great deal more than peanuts. But as an overall rule, every single no-limit player in the world who's dependent entirely on his poker winnings for a living will end up broke from time to time. The good *limit* poker player, on the other hand, as long as he plays with the percentages in his favor and lets no one bet enough in one fell swoop to break him will keep on increasing his bankroll as his mathematical advantage works for him over the passage of time, and if he's prudent in his living habits he should always stay in money. Alas, the last sentence is the rub; most fine limit players aren't prudent in their living habits, and those are the people you'll see dealing in card rooms or working menial jobs from time to time in order to get together a poker-playing grubstake.

I've also heard all the arguments on the other side as to no-limit players and their capabilities. Tales of player/psychics who can read players to the point that they know their opponents' hole cards make excellent filler material for ESPN announcers, and although I'll acknowledge that anyone with that much insight should never lose, I don't believe that such a person exists. If Brunson and Hellmuth and Lederer and Negreanu and whoever always know what their opponents have in the pocket, then why do I see them calling so many bets when they're beaten? I believe that after playing with someone over a period of months, or even years, a good player learns his or her opponent's general betting habits, but stories of "picking up tells" on players after watching them for only a few hands are unfounded urban legends. You're never going to shake my belief regarding no-limit poker, and far be it for me to try to change yours, and if after reading this you still think no-limit poker is the way to go, feel free. If you do go the no-limit route, however, don't follow in the footsteps of several poker all-Americans and come to me for

a loan when your bankroll disappears. I won't help you finan-
cially, but I will remind you that I told you so.

Before I used up so many pages on limit and no-limit playing strategies, I was about to tell you about my Las Vegas experience, and though it may seem that I've taken some unnecessary
detours, I do have a purpose in mind. Before a poker player even
thinks about taking on Nevada, if he's going to have a chance
out there he's got to develop and fine-tune his game to a level
that few ever achieve, and anyone heading for Las Vegas before
he's ready is courting disaster. Before my first trip ever to Las
Vegas I'd pretty well mastered—if one ever masters anything having to do with the game called Hold 'Em—the playing chops
required, but I didn't have a clue as to self-management and
discipline. I did go out west and, after first learning a painful
series of lessons, survive for quite a while, but I'm certain that
I would've been many dollars better off if I'd remained in Dallas, where I belonged. I'm a much better poker player because
of the time I spent in Nevada, but was the Las Vegas experience
worth what it cost me? I think I'll just tell what happened and
let you be the judge.

The weeklong trip that eventually stretched into a decade,
give or take, began with an invitation from a guy to go on a
vacation with him. He was an on-again, off-again stockbroker
I'd first met in college who spent more time in the backroom
Dallas card rooms than he did servicing accounts and keeping
up with the markets. During one wee-hour breakfast after a night-
long poker session, he suggested that the two of us fly to Las
Vegas the following day, catch a few shows, and play a little poker
to cover our traveling expenses. Frankly, I was more than a little
bit leery; not only was my buddy a consistent big loser in the
poker game, but he was also under investigation by the SEC for
using clients' stock certificates as collateral for some of his own

personal loans. Within the next couple of years he was headed for a stretch in federal prison, and looking back on things from today's perspective, I'm shocked at myself for letting the lure of Nevada get the best of me. I'd been having an excellent run of cards and my pockets were full of folding money. And I'd been hearing tales of Las Vegas action for years, though the guys telling the stories had usually just returned home from Nevada and were looking for a grubstake loan. I remember sitting in a booth at the Toddle House—an all-night greasy spoon chain with locations all over hell and gone in those days—eating bacon and eggs along with my stockbroker buddy and thinking, "What the hell," and the very next evening we were on our way.

For the benefit of my younger readership, I think I should explain how such a whirlwind trip came to be, since today it wouldn't be possible unless you were so rich that you didn't need to play poker for income; in the early 1970s, there was no such thing as a cheap two-week advance ticket purchase, and security gates and metal detectors at airports were still a few years away—D. B. Cooper hadn't yet bailed from a Northwest Orient flight with a suitcase full of cash, and Osama bin Laden was fourteen years old at the time. To travel to Las Vegas we walked up to the Delta ticket counter, paid for our tickets in cash, checked our suitcases, and walked aboard the jetliner without so much as giving our names. We chose the ten P.M. departure because the redeye was a half-fare flight, and our round-trip tickets were something like seventy bucks apiece. Airliners flew a lot faster in those days, because the fuel crunch of the mid-1970s hadn't come to pass, and with the two-hour time difference between Texas and Nevada taken into consideration, we took off at ten and landed at nine-thirty, Las Vegas time.

Las Vegas landings are old hat to me now, but I'll never forget that first touchdown at McCarran Field (now an international airport but then sort of a one-horse operation; Las Vegas's

population was only about 150,000 at the time), the Strip less
than a mile away on our left; the dazzling neon at the Sands,
the Dunes, the Sahara, and the Trop lighting up the desert like
noontime; the addictive *ching-ching* of the airport terminal slot
machines audible the second we left the plane, the sounds send-
ing adrenaline pumping through our veins. My stockbroker buddy
changed a five-dollar bill, lost the entire five in about ten minutes, and was headed back for more change when I grabbed him
by the arm and hauled him off to the baggage claim.

The day we'd left Dallas I'd called an old poker player who
was a Las Vegas veteran and asked the guy for a recommenda-
tion on a place to stay. The guy had referred me to a motel/room-
ing house on East Ogden Street, a block west of and around
the corner from the Golden Nugget Gambling Hall. The Golden
Nugget stood in the same place as it does today, across the street
from the Horseshoe and Four Queens casinos, and catty-cornered
from the Fremont, the four casinos situated at the intersection
of Fremont Street and Las Vegas Boulevard, the most famous
corner in the gambling world. There was no hotel attached to
the Nugget in those days, and since the main Las Vegas poker
action went on in the Nugget (a famous old stud player named
Bill Boyd was the Nugget's room manager; Boyd was the first
to recognize and tap the money to be made in poker rooms featuring Hold 'Em, and for several years, he had the Las Vegas poker
business all to himself), and since the ten-dollar rate at the rooming house was the best deal going, there wasn't any decision to
be made regarding accommodations as far as I was concerned.
But my stockbroker friend had other ideas; the guy wanted to
get a luxury suite at the Sands, for Christ's sake, and we argued
all the way downtown in a taxicab about where we were going
to stay. I finally convinced him to try the rooming house, at
least to the point of stowing his luggage in the room I was going
to rent, and after we'd checked out the action at the Nugget he

could then take his belongings to the Sands if he wanted to. Frankly, by the time we reached the intersection of Fremont Street and Las Vegas Boulevard, I was chomping at the bit to get rid of the guy. We got out of the cab amid blazing neon and schlepped our luggage around the corner to the rooming house.

The room was about the size of your average college dormitory pad and there was a community shower down the hall, but it was clean as a whistle and for ten bucks a night a five-minute walk from some of the best poker action in the country, so who was complaining? Well, in truth, my buddy was, but by that time I'd pretty well tuned him out. We stowed our gear in the room, walked around the corner, did some rubbernecking of the most brightly lit street in the world, and walked into the Golden Nugget. I took about four steps inside the entry and stopped in my tracks, my stockbroker friend bumping into me from the rear.

You can say all you want about advances in technology, but the modern generation of gamblers who never saw the casinos of yesteryear doesn't know what it's missing. Today's gambling palaces with their noiseless computerized slot machines, the ones that pay off in slips of paper that the winner can redeem at the cashier's cage, are no doubt more efficient and secure and easier on the eardrums, but nothing will ever replace the jackpot bell that could be heard for blocks, the *ching-ching* and clatter of coins sliding into the trays, the click of the handles on the one-armed bandits, and the absolute funhouse atmosphere of the old-time joints. Beyond the slots, the table games were visible and the players were elbow to elbow and wall to wall, blackjack dealers expertly shuffling and dealing from single decks, stickmen at the crap tables chanting their endless monotones: *Seven away, seven, good for the don'ts, bad for the pass-line bettors, a new roller, a new bowler, bet seven, eleven, or any craps, dice are comin' out*... I stood there hypnotized, rooted in my tracks, until the stockbroker tapped me on the shoulder. I turned around to face the guy.

"What are we gonna play?" he said.

His question puzzled me. We'd never discussed playing any game but poker on this trip. I looked to the back of the casino, slightly to my left, at the sign overhead reading "Poker." I gestured. "Our game's back there."

"I'm thinking maybe I oughtta try a little twenty-one," he said.

I studied him closely. His pupils were shiny, his mouth slack. You can tell a lot about people by watching their arrival in a place like Las Vegas; the ones who reach for their money before they even leave the airport and who upon glimpsing a row of blackjack and dice tables fidget around as if a herd of ants has invaded their underwear have a problem and shouldn't go within a hundred miles of a casino. I hadn't yet learned to pick out the addicts, but I was about to get my first valuable lesson. "Blackjack?" I said. "Not me. I'm going to the poker room."

"Yeah, well." He stood first on one foot and then the other. "I'll meet you there in a minute. I'm gonna take a little detour." He left me and hustled off toward the blackjack tables.

There was a prickly sensation at the back of my neck as I watched him go. But what the hell, I hadn't adopted the guy and he could do as he pleased. I wound my way through the crowd, nearly colliding with a slot machine change girl in a short skirt and mesh hose, and entered my first-ever Las Vegas card room.

Hold 'Em hadn't quite taken over the poker world as yet; there was a Razz table and a seven-card stud table in addition to four tables dealing strictly Hold 'Em, with limits from one and two dollars all the way up to ten and twenty (and for everyone who thinks ten and twenty is a cheap game, remember that this all happened over thirty years ago; ten and twenty was about the biggest limit game going back then, though occasionally the Nugget would open up a twenty-and-forty table when certain high players were around). I'd never seen house dealers until that moment—or oblong poker tables, either, as a matter of fact; in the illegal joints back home we still played pass-the-deal on round tables padded with sponge—and I stood there mesmerized for a minute, watching the Hold 'Em action until I felt I had the hang of it. I knew from the old pros in Dallas about the button and what it meant, though I'd never seen the button in person, and I watched in fascination as the dealer slid the chip decorated with a triangle around the table to indicate who had last action in the next hand dealt. Waiting lists I knew about; we even had waiting lists back in Texas, so I approached the sign-in counter and added my name to the ten-and-twenty list, noted that my name was third down the line, then sat down at an empty poker table with a half dozen other players who were waiting for a seat, just as I was. There was one fortyish woman with graying hair in the group; I remember her because I'd never seen a woman in a poker parlor except for the drink and food servers. The men were scruffy western types in plaid shirts and jeans, most with five o'clock shadows, one with a full-fledged beard. The woman was stocky with very large hands.

I recognized Bill Boyd as he entered the poker room and went behind the counter; I'd seen pictures of him, and once, a few years earlier, he'd visited and played in Dallas at the Amvets Club, though at the time I was in the limit game and he'd played with the big boys at the no-limit table, and I was pretty sure that Boyd wouldn't know me from Adam. I suspected that I could drop a few names—Bob Hooks, Cowboy Wolford, Bill Smith, men I now played with regularly back in Dallas—and that Boyd would welcome me with open arms, though even at that early stage in my poker career I didn't think it a good idea to advertise myself and where I came from. Boyd was a smallish, slightly stooped man in his sixties with short, nearly white hair parted on the left. Over the next decade I was to get to know Bill Boyd quite well. In the not too distant future he was to turn a trick that no one else had before or has since: winning the five-card stud prelim at the World Series of Poker five years in a row. No one has ever won five consecutive bracelets in the same event, and I'd bet a lot of money that no one ever will again. Five-card stud is a lost art today and no longer a WSOP event, but I still think it's the toughest poker game ever invented and takes the most skill to play successfully. Game runners were glad to see five-card stud fade into oblivion, because the players did a lot of studying and chin scratching and each hand took seemingly forever to finish, but poker players with Bill Boyd's talents come along only once in a generation or so.

As I sat there waiting for a ten-and-twenty seat, I watched the game in progress fifteen feet away from me, and the prospects of my sitting down in the game anytime soon were pretty dismal. People on poker room waiting lists might look like civilized folk in pleasant conversation as they sit together at a not-in-use table, but don't let outward appearances fool you; there is no more vicious pack of vultures in the world. They shoot glances at the table they're waiting for a seat to join and keep track of players' chip stacks like auditing CPAs. The regular, everyday Waiting List Gang knows the habits of every player in the game down to the size of each player's bankroll, and as the stack in front of certain players diminishes, the vultures circle nearer and nearer, knowing that when Sammy Sucker goes all in and his chips disappear, he's through for that session and one of the vultures can claim his seat. The Waiting List Gang also knows the deep-pocketed players who if they lose the stacks in front of them will pull out more money and keep on playing for the duration, and the vultures pay little attention to those players, because counting them down is a waste of time. But when Sammy Sucker happens to win a big one to stave off certain doom, the vultures sometimes mutter out loud among themselves. I'd never seen any of the players before, of course, so I had no way of predicting who'd be first to fall, but after listening to the comments from the Waiting List Gang I had a pretty good idea.

An hour passed before the first ten-and-twenty seat came open, making me second in line, and it occurred to me that I might have to go get some sleep and wait for tomorrow to play. It was nearly midnight, Las Vegas time, so back in Dallas it was approaching two in the morning, and I found myself stifling a few yawns. I'd just stood up and stretched and sat back down when I had the sensation that someone was watching me. I looked around the card room, then let my gaze wander to the casino floor.

And there stood my stockbroker buddy, gesturing wildly in my direction. It was at that moment that I quit thinking of him as my buddy and silently anointed him the pain in the ass that he was.

I went into the casino and met the stockbroker in the general vicinity of the Big Wheel. As the wheel spun and clicked he nervously licked his lips. "Look, could you let me have a little money?" he said, then looked hopeful and added, "I'll pay interest."

I'm no loan shark. I would've gotten mad, I suppose, if he hadn't looked so pitiful. "Jesus," I said, "you've already lost your bankroll?"

"Just until we get back home." He folded his arms and hugged himself.

I studied my feet. I shook my head. I didn't know how much he'd lost, but when we'd boarded the plane he'd been carrying a pretty thick roll of hundred-dollar bills. I lifted my chin until

I was nose to nose with him. "Follow me," I said, then walked fast toward the exit.

He trailed me by a couple of steps, all the way out of the Nugget, catty-cornered across the intersection to the sidewalk that ran in front of the Fremont, down to the end of the block, and around the corner to the rooming house on East Odgen. I unlocked the door and took him inside the room, then dug five twenty-dollar bills out of my pocket, and finally pointed at his luggage. "Get your gear," I told him.

He regarded me wildly as if I could either let him have the money or have the life choked out of me.

I held the five twenties out. "Here's what I'm going to do," I said. "I'm giving you a hundred dollars and I don't expect you to pay me back. But I want you out of my room. If you're smart you'll catch a taxi to the airport and get on the next flight back to Dallas, but you're a grown man and I can't tell you what to do. I think you've got a gambling problem and need some help. Whatever, I'm also not your shrink. But this hundred is it. If you don't leave town and you lose this money in some casino, don't bother looking for me for any more, because I won't give it to you."

Ten minutes later I stood beside him on the curb as his taxi arrived and even helped the cab driver throw his luggage in the trunk. As the cab pulled away, the stockbroker hung his head and wouldn't look at me. I never saw the guy again, but I did hear a few years later that he was living on the street, so I don't guess my words of wisdom had much effect. As I walked the block and a half back to the Golden Nugget, I had twinges of conscience over the way I'd treated the guy, but scenes such as the ones I'd just played are part of the life, and I might just as well learn to get any feelings of guilt out of my mind. If you play a lot of poker you'll encounter gambling addicts on a pretty regular basis; it's a downer, but it's really no sadder a sight than the desperation shown by the credit abusers of the business world. I know lots of pros who seek out addicts and take them for everything, including their rent and food money, but I steer clear of really hooked gamblers whenever I can. I won't play with drunks either, and I've gotten my share of criticism from other players when I've cashed in and left whenever some guy has a few too many and starts throwing his money around, but personally I rate poker players who take advantage of drunks and addicts right along with muggers who beat up cripples. Then again, that may be the reason I'm the pigeon and those other players are the pros.

As far as your own propensity for gambling addiction goes, you simply have to take personal inventory before striking off down any sort of path as a poker player. My own self-evaluation is this: I don't bet on sports. I don't play roulette or bet on the big wheel, though I do take a turn at the crap table—Titanic Thompson's system, remember?—just about every time I pass through a casino and I'm many dollars ahead of the dice and expect to continue to be. Horse racing bores me to death and I won't go to the track except under protest, and once there I see plenty of action at the two-dollar window. I will play blackjack occasionally, but I have a little system for that as well, and once I lose my preset limit, I never let the door hit me in the ass as I'm getting out of there. When playing poker I quit immediately after a series of bad beats gets my blood in an uproar, and I never continue to play when I might be on tilt. I also carry a preset amount to every game and never exceed my limit in any one session, and I know very fine players who disagree with that strategy; my old buddy Junior Hess, for example, won't quit as long as the game is in progress and believes that if he sits there long enough he'll come out ahead in the end. If that method works for Junior, more power to him, but that's not my MO and never will be.

Oh, and as for my first night ever in Las Vegas? As it turned out, I never got to play. Originally I'd sat through an hour when only one player quit the ten-and-twenty game, yet during the fifteen minutes it took for me to walk around the corner and load the stockbroker and his suitcase into a cab, my spot on the waiting list had come and gone and there were now five on the list ahead of me. I decided that I'd had it for that day, and that I'd wait until I'd slept to tackle the Golden Nugget's poker room. I went back to the rooming house and went to bed, and spent a long time staring at the ceiling in anger because of the street noise right outside my door. Over the next decade I'd get used to the noise, and even today my wife swears that I could sleep through World War II. And you know what? She's right; downtown Las Vegas has to be the loudest place in the world, twenty-four/seven, and if I could sleep through the racket of the Gambling Mecca of the World, I could probably sleep just as soundly with tanks firing missiles over my head.

8

MAKING DO IN NEVADA

or,
The Life and Times of the Golden Nugget Kid

Monkey One prodded me with the shotgun twice on the way down the corridor and into the living room, and each time he did so I closed my eyes, sure that my next breath would be my last one. Finally, I stepped out of the hall and onto the living room shag carpet. Here the odor of burnt gunpowder was strong enough to burn my nostrils. On my right, the easy chair beside the sofa had a black hole blown in its back about two feet in diameter, and the wall behind the chair was blackened as well. "Fuckin' hair trigger," Monkey One said, then prodded me from behind once more and added, "Turn around and look at me."

I did a very slow about-face. If the guy removed his mask so that I could see his face, I'd be done for no matter what, and I made up my mind that if that was the case I was making a run for it. The guy could shoot me before I made it halfway to the door, but I was grasping at straws here.

Monkey One still wore the chimpanzee mask. I breathed a sigh of relief.

Monkey One said, "That your Eldo parked at the bottom of the steps?"

It was; since I was always the first to arrive at the poker game, I always parked in the same spot nose on to the bottom step leading up to the apartment. Since the hijackers apparently knew my car by sight, they'd spent a while keeping track of me when casing the job. I'd bought the year-old Cadillac after a really profitable Las Vegas trip just a couple of months earlier. I told Monkey One, my voice breaking in fear, that the Eldo was indeed my car.

"Okay," he said, "here's what you're gonna do. See them two bags?"

There were two gunnysacks on the floor beside the front door. I nodded.

"You're gonna take them bags downstairs and load 'em in the trunk of your car. If you see anybody walkin' around down there, grin and say hidy. We'll be watchin' from the window, and if you do anything but load the bags and get your ass back upstairs, we'll go in the back and shoot somebody. And if we shoot one, we might just as well kill 'em all. You got that?"

I nodded that I got it but, at the same time, felt a little bit puzzled. If they were going to steal my car, why not just strip me of my keys and leave? Finally I got it. If anyone was gonna be stopped leaving the apartment with two sacks full of money, it wasn't gonna be Monkey One or Monkey Two. Also, if they stayed hidden as they watched me load the car, they could be certain that there was no one lurking near my vehicle intent on stopping them from making their getaway. I hated these hijackers and was pretty sure that I could kill both of them without blinking, but I had to admit that they were far from stupid.

I picked up the sacks and, one dangling heavily from each hand, went out on the landing as Monkey Two held the door open. The door closed softly behind me, and I started down the steps. I was

walking as lightly as I possibly could, but in the heavy silence my
footsteps sounded loud enough to puncture eardrums.

Trying to make a living playing poker in Las Vegas during the 1970s and '80s wasn't what it was cracked up to be, even when you were winning, and when you were losing, the life sucked big-time. Since poker players as a rule didn't play casino games such as craps and blackjack, and since casino bosses were still years away from waking up to the profits available from slot machines and poker games, perks such as comped hotel rooms, food, shows, hookers, and whatnot simply didn't exist even for the famous high-player types who frequented casino card rooms. The house would furnish drinks in the poker room as long as you were playing, but there was even a rub to that freebie; poker players in their right minds didn't drink alcohol at the table, and if you'd been paying for soft drinks or coffee the price was only a quarter. As long as you were playing poker the cocktail waitresses would keep the refreshments coming free of charge, but if you failed to toss the waitress a chip on delivery she'd forget your order the next time. Since the cheapest chip at the ten-and-twenty table was worth a dollar, you were better off taking a break from the action every so often and schlepping your own drinks over from the bar after you bought them. Such practice didn't make you really popular with the waitress set, but since those young ladies were in it strictly for the dollar, you were better off not knowing any of them to begin with. I had two good friends who married cocktail waitresses in Las Vegas. One woke up the morning after the wedding to find his money gone along with his wife, and the other will spend the rest of his life in a wheelchair because of an incident where he caught his wife with another man.

As for meals: You could get the ninety-nine-cent breakfast offered at several downtown casinos, and eat it family style right alongside the nickel roulette players and two-bit crap shooters, but since a professional poker player attending to business was up all night most of the time, the breakfast-serving hours of nine to eleven in the morning didn't fit in with the pro's sleep schedule very well. The Sombrero Room at the Horseshoe served really fine Tex-Mex food, and Yosemite Sam's and a Chinese joint in the Nugget lobby cooked up really good crab melts and delicious chicken lo mein, but those were the upscale restaurants and pretty damned expensive. The affordable menus at the Mint, Silver Slipper, and Lucky Dollar downtown were strictly greasy spoon, and existing on a diet of cheeseburgers and French fries wasn't really good for the digestive system, but that was pretty much what was available to us as long as we stayed where the action was. After a few months in Las Vegas, I located a cafeteria in a strip shopping center far from the gambling district and hoofed the two miles once a week for a balanced meal, and if it hadn't been for the cafeteria food I don't think I would have survived. Some players went through rigid workout regimens in an effort to stay sharp, and while I don't doubt that workouts would have helped, they'd never been my bag and I wasn't about to change.

There were, of course, other ways to stay awake for the three or four days that many pros believed were necessary to make a living. Drugs were everywhere up and down the Strip, and on downtown's Casino Row, coke and speed were as plentiful as booze. It was sort of an unwritten rule in Sin City that while law enforcement policed the business and residential areas like bloodhounds, the drug and prostitution business that went on in the gambling joints went largely ignored. Often nighttime customers at Caesar's Palace and the Hilton couldn't find a seat at the bar because there was a hooker on every stool, and I've lost count of the times that I entered the Nugget's men's room to find guys doing lines of coke at the sink, right out in the open, with the restroom attendant furnishing razor blades and straws right along with cologne and aftershave. I had many friends who got hooked on drugs and have stayed that way; Stu Ungar, the threetime WSOP Main Event champion, died from an overdose the year after his third victory, and 1979 WSOP Main Event second place finisher Bobby (the Wizard) Hoff will be the first to tell you that cocaine is largely responsible for the downward spirals he's had in his career from time to time. I knew another Big-Time Poker Guy from Texas who stood naked as a jaybird on the Nugget's roof tossing wadded hundred-dollar bills into the street like confetti, and this particular guy finally had to leave Nevada in order to regain his sanity. Apparently, the Las Vegas drug trade hasn't slowed one iota over the past three decades; I saw cocaine in major amounts in casino restrooms as late as July of 2006.

If you could maintain a healthy lifestyle, avoid the drugs, and steer clear of the hookers, there was money to be made at the poker tables. Back in Texas, I'd made it a practice to play only during the day, in order to avoid the cheats and muggers, but because the Golden Nugget poker room was safe and secure—police laxity didn't extend to hijackers, because robberies were a hindrance to the gambling trade, and out-and-out cheating simply didn't go on in Las Vegas card rooms—and because it was after sundown when the tourists came out to howl, I became pretty much of a night creature.

But I did make it a practice to sleep eight hours out of every twenty-four on most days, and at least six hours on the days when I didn't put in the full eight. I left my room every night at nine on the dot; walked the block and a half to the Golden Nugget; and no matter how much I was losing or how little I was ahead, I quit the game at six A.M. And, yes, I know that my playing habits were a lot different from those of most professionals. Poker gurus say that the only factor determining a professional's quitting time is the quality of the game—whether it's a fast and fairly loose game with sizeable pots, or a tightass game where trying to win is like pulling teeth—and that as long as the game stays good the pro should keep his or her seat no matter what.

And who's right, me or the play-til-you-drop advocates? I've got no idea, actually, and I suppose the answer lies in the individual's physical makeup. During my early days in Las Vegas, I found that if I played more than nine hours a day my mind wandered to the point that I couldn't concentrate on the game, and that if I stayed and played for too long I became just another sucker ripe to have his pocket picked. There were a few guys whose games didn't seem to suffer even when they sat up night after night without sleep, but those players were the ones snorting the coke and popping the pills. I'd made up my mind to steer clear of drugs, and with that goal firmly in mind, I made up my own rules as to when I should or shouldn't play.

I played poker regularly in Las Vegas for ten years without losing my sanity or my bankroll, but I doubt that I could've had as much success as I did if I'd moved to Nevada and become a permanent resident. The four months that I spent in the rooming house on East Ogden during my very first trip out west was my longest consecutive stretch in Las Vegas, and I was never without a Dallas hat-hanging pad. Since I spent a full third of my time—maybe closer to half, the more I think about it—in Las Vegas playing at the Golden Nugget, I'm sure most of the local players thought I lived there full-time, but every month I'd go home for a week or two in order to keep my engine revved. When in Las Vegas I practically lived in the poker room when I wasn't eating or sleeping, but on my trips to Dallas I did other things and pushed the game of poker out of my mind. And since the only time they ever saw me that decade was during their own trips out west, my old buddies at the Amvets Club thought

I'd moved to Las Vegas as well, and I told them nothing to set them straight. I was a regular customer at the East Ogden rooming house—where I watched the rent go from ten bucks a day to fifteen, and then to twenty—until it closed in 1976, and after that I stayed in a series of Las Vegas's most inexpensive motels: Day's Inns, Red Roof Inns, and the like, places without casinos where a man could have his privacy. I lived a very lonely existence in Las Vegas, and looking back on my time there and seeing what's happened to some other poker players that I knew, I'm glad that I didn't make many friends out there.

As you might imagine, adjusting to Las Vegas poker games required a change in playing strategy, though not the kind of change you'd expect. I've seen a lot of good Hold 'Em players show up in Las Vegas and, because they believe the rumors and think they're really up against it, suddenly change their game plans and play very conservatively. I was guilty of the same error when I first came to Nevada, and it took me a couple of weeks to get the lay of the land, and with thirty years of Las Vegas play to look back on, I can say with confidence that in order to win in Nevada, you've got to play looser than you ever have.

Notice that I said "play looser," not "play dumber." There's a big difference. Playing loose doesn't mean playing stupid, though the more you can give the *appearance* of playing stupid without actually doing so, the better off you'll be. And once I got my game tuned in to Las Vegas action, I discovered something that I never would have believed: *It was actually easier to win in Nevada games than in the back-alley card rooms in Texas. Whazzat?* you say.

You heard me, and now I'll elaborate. If you have read *Play Poker Like a Pigeon* you know that I advocated steering clear of Las Vegas and its shark-filled waters in that book, and that's still the advice I'm giving today, but that's now and I'm talking about the situation then. Today you can find legal card rooms in almost every state, and no one lives more than a four-hour drive from the nearest poker game, and the country's softest legal action goes on far away from Las Vegas. When I first went to Nevada it was the only state with casino gambling (though California and Montana offered certain forms of Mickey Mouse poker that a real player wouldn't stoop to) and other than the back-street games that went on in just about every major city, Las Vegas was pretty much "it" for medium- to high-stakes Hold 'Em. Legal card rooms were the safest and best places to play back in the '70s, just as they are today, and while—late at night, at any rate—about half the seats at the table in a Las Vegas game might hold tougher competitors than you'd find back home, the butts of some of the softest players imaginable filled the remaining chairs. So although the following is a lesson on the difference between private play and play in casino poker rooms, and although I'll talk strictly about my Las Vegas experience, the strategy I'm advocating will be the same in any legal card room in the world. It's an odd phenomenon that players who play in a weekly game with "the gang" in their home town imagine themselves poker sharks, and when in Las Vegas they steer clear of the "sucker" games like craps and blackjack in favor of the games where they honestly believe they are a favorite to win. The truth is just the opposite; the average Las Vegas tourist would have a better chance shooting craps than he or she does up against the school of barracudas at the Hold 'Em table, but you'll never convince Mr. or Mrs. Tourist of that fact and it's a waste of time to try.

Not that playing in a game with five clueless sheep doesn't have its pitfalls; those folks are apt to play with any two-card combination, and once the flop appears, they're going to draw at about any hand that has the remotest chance of winning, and there will be times when those players will draw out on you until they make you want to puke. And that's why you need more stake money (say, about twice the amount that you're accustomed to bringing) in order to play in such a game, and even though you're a much greater favorite to win against this sort of competition than you are in a game populated by competent Hold 'Em players, you're going to go through some pretty drastic fluctuations in your bankroll before the odds finally work out for you.

And as for playing loose but not dumb, in a game like the one I'm describing it's hard to loosen up while maintaining control and not just playing like the rest of the suckers. Position play is not nearly as critical in this game as it is in a tougher environment, because none of the weakos are playing position, and you can forget about any hand analysis based on where the bettor sits in relation to the button. Furthermore, any position moves of your own such as stealing the button or raising with a less than pristine hand in order to disguise your pocket cards are absolute wastes of time, because once the hand moves on past the flop, the really weak players won't remember who raised when and will attach no significance to the raise even if they do. Even if you're on the button, none of the weak players are going to assess any raises on your part any differently than if you had the big or small blind. You can play hands in early position that you wouldn't normally come in with, since should the board hit these hands your payoff will be just as huge whether you're in last position or in the blind, and with constant five-to-one action for your money, it simply pays to take those suited connectors and small pairs and run with them no matter where you're sitting. Position play is wasted on weak players in the same way that brush blocking is wasted on a three-hundred pound lineman who has his ears pinned back and is charging the quarterback; any finesse on your part will just get you run over and trampled on. In this game, you raise before the flop only if you think you have the best hand and want more money in the pot. Any pre-flop raise merely to eliminate players is pointless, because these folks are going to see the flop regardless of what you do, and once those first three cards hit the board you'd best take your AA or KK, grab hold of your ass with both hands, and get ready for a pretty rough ride. The weak player will come at you just as strongly with top pair as with the nuts, and it will never occur to him or her that you might be holding an over-pair no matter what your actions before the flop. You play big pairs in this game under the theory that they'll stand up often enough to make you come out far ahead, and in a really weak game it's impossible to know when to get away from those big two-card hands the way you can in a game where the players know what they're doing.

I know good players who say they'd rather play against professionals than weakos because it's so hard to put the sucker on a hand, and though I strongly disagree with that sentiment, I can see where the good players are coming from. In truth, I probably lost more often in individual poker sessions in Las Vegas than I did in the games back home, but my winning turns in the card room brought in so much more money than I'd ever dreamed of that the losing sessions didn't matter all that much. Eventually I had so much cash lying around that I worried continually about thieves making off with my bankroll, so I opened bank accounts, which brought the IRS into play. And after losing a lot of sleep worrying about tax liens and whatnot, I finally applied for a federal gambling stamp and started making quarterly self-employment deposits and filing pretty accurate tax returns, and it's still my practice to do so today. I've seen Uncle Sam bring down many gambling professionals, and it's such an ugly sight that I believe anyone planning to make all or a portion of his or her income at the poker table is a fool to do anything other than pay taxes right on down the line.

I had several role models in Las Vegas whom I learned from, which I couldn't have done today, because card rooms such as the one at the Bellagio keep the poker elite (and I translate "poker elite" as follows: the players with more money than sense who play for ridiculous sums) separated from the hoi polloi to the point that someone wanting to learn from the top pros can never get close enough to watch their favorites in action. In olden times, the big-name pros were first and foremost poker players making a living at the game (as opposed to today, where the stars all have book deals, online poker room endorsement deals, and televised, no-risk tournament deals with the TV producers furnishing the bankroll), and if the Golden Nugget had the only action in town on a given day, and the Nugget's biggest game was twenty- and forty-dollar limit, then that's where the all-stars would lay their money down. I've run into Bob Hooks at the Nugget—in fact, he was a card room greeter working for Bill Boyd for a while—as well as Brunson, Johnny Moss, Chip Reese, Johnny Chan, David Chiu, Bobby Hoff, and countless other pros whose names you might not recognize but whose games were every bit as feared as the marquee guys'. David Chiu was probably the best limit player in Las Vegas back then, but Johnny Chan won more money in the Nugget's limit games than anyone. Chan was the most aggressive limit player I ever saw. To emulate the guy, you'd have to scare up plenty of bankroll to stay in the game long enough for your style to take effect, but copying Chan might be the best thing you could do to win in the long run.

Chan was a real study, a work in progress that was rough around the edges at the time, but he was blessed with such incredible card sense that he won despite making some mistakes that would've sent a normal man home as broke as a toad. His MO was to buy about four times as many chips as anyone else at the table—I've seen him pull out a thousand dollars to play ten and twenty more than once—and then do his best to bully the game into submission. And his strategy worked, especially against the weak players, because Chan had his opponents so gun-shy that some of them would start tossing in their hands the second he reached for his chips. Actually, the best way to handle Johnny Chan in a limit game was to call him down with any hand at all—such as top pair, and to hell with your kicker—the problem being that the weaker players' definition of "any hand at all" included second or third pair, or some sort of half-assed middle-buster straight draw; and coming at Chan with any of that garbage was certain suicide. Often Chan bluffed with possibilities—bluffed, in other words, with some sort of legitimate draw like an open-ended straight or flush—and if both Chan and his opponent happened to miss their draws, Chan would bet and steal the pot at the end. The really stunning facet of Chan's game was his ability to know his opponents and exactly where he stood at every point in every hand, and the adjustments he made in his game depending on the strength of the opposition. The man never forgot any move by any player, and if you tried some strategy that worked once against Chan, you could forget about ever using the same ploy again, because he wouldn't go for it a second time.

Once upon a time, I won a pot from Chan by checking from early position and then calling him down when he bet, and showing him top pair at the end to drag the money after he'd bluffed off a hundred dollars or so. A few days later I played an identical pot against him in the same manner only this time when I checked it to him after the flop he refused to bet, and then when I led with a bet on Fourth Street, he tossed in his hand as if the cards were on fire. I tried all sorts of different strategies against Chan, all to no avail, and I finally conceded that the only way to beat him was to join him, and after that, unless I had a really big hand I simply refused to play in a pot with the guy. Johnny Chan, for a really top player always in control, did the best imitation of a wild man I've ever seen, and I continue to think he was an even better limit poker player than he ever was at no-limit, even though today he has two Main Event bracelets to his credit.

Which is more than I can say for Brunson, Reese, Hooks, and most of the other big names; as a matter of fact, when any of those guys had to contend with a betting limit, I thought their overall play was pretty ordinary. No-limit players stuck in a limit game tend to use one of two styles: some become call-every-bet-and-bluff-your-money-off-when-they-check-to-you suckers (I've heard no-limit players rationalize that they're so used to playing for sky-high stakes that the sums wagered in limit poker become insignificant, and that's the reason they throw their bankroll away; I don't personally buy into that argument, because in fifteen- and thirty- or thirty- and sixty-dollar limit, five-thousand-dollar wins and losses are commonplace, and any player who loses *five thousand dollars* playing poker and calls that amount chickenfeed is either lying or crazy) while others retreat into Sklansky mode (1970s Sklansky and not the improved model of today) and become such tightwads that they have little or no chance to win.

In the early 1980s, Amarillo Slim Preston hosted two tournaments called the Amarillo Slim Super Bowl of Poker, held at the Sahara Reno one year and the Sahara Tahoe the next, and during the Reno stint someone set up a $500 and $1,000 limit game with $250 and $500 blinds, strictly to showcase all of the high rollers for the benefit of the tournament attendees. All of the players involved were basically no-limit guys (Brunson played, along with Bobby Baldwin, Chip Reese, Amarillo Slim himself, Sailor Roberts, and Cowboy Wolford, to name a few), but the game organizers set the table up center stage on the casino floor and allowed spectators to gather around like flies. Among the railbirds were some of the best limit poker players alive, and after they'd watched the fiasco unfolding before them for an hour or so, those professional limit players began to drool. The play at the table was really that bad, and before long you could see groups of good limit players forming to discuss pooling resources. The problem was the amount of the buy-in; although anyone in the room could take a seat in the game if he had $5,000, five grand in a game like that was hardly enough to play once around the table. Just about every good limit poker player agrees that one should have access to a minimum of twenty times the larger of the two limits ($20,000 in a $500- and $1,000-limit game, in other words) before taking a seat, and although many of the limit players present had that amount and more in their pockets, no limit player in his right mind was going to risk twenty grand in a game where, if he was unlucky enough to lose in this one and only session, he likely wouldn't be able to find another 500-and-1,000 game anytime soon where he could get his money back. Some of us finally pooled the twenty grand—personally I came across with $500—and backed a young limit poker whiz from Texas against the marquee guys, and each one of us realized several times our investment as a profit. This was all many years ago, of course, and time has dulled my memory as to the exact amounts won or lost—the only figure that stands out is a hundred grand, the amount that Cowboy Wolford lost of his brother Ray's money—but, suffice to say, the profit from that one game paid my trip expenses from Dallas to Reno and back many times over, and I never had to take a seat at the table or look at a card.

I once asked a really fine limit poker player to describe his dream game to me. He thought for a minute, then grinned, pointed to his left, and said, "Doyle over there," then pointed to his right and said, "Dewey over there" (referring to another Big-Time Poker Guy named Dewey Tomko). "And Johnny Moss, right over there," he added as he scratched his head and pointed straight ahead.

And with the limit player's comments as a lead-in, I'll now translate our little secret into a postulate: **Big-name no-limit** poker players are, as a rule, helpless in a limit game, and the one exception I've ever seen to that rule is Johnny Chan. I should add that some modern young big-timers have reputations as excellent limit players as well, but I've been away from the Las Vegas arena for so long that I've never played with any of them, so I can't really comment one way or the other on their skills.

And as for Las Vegas's ballyhooed no-limit games, during the ten years that I was in Las Vegas practically year-round, I don't recall no-limit poker being offered in a single casino card room unless (1) it was a special set-up affair featuring big-name poker players and designed to attract spectators, or (2) the game went on during WSOP time. It's an odd fact—though no more odd than lots of facts having to do with the game of poker and its history—that although Benny Binnion, the Horseshoe's late owner, is rightfully credited with having invented the World Series of Poker, the Horseshoe itself was too cramped for space to offer poker twelve months a year. Today the WSOP is a summertime affair lasting several months, with all but the vary tail end of the tournament held at the Rio; in the 1970s and '80s, however, the poker room at the Horseshoe was open from early February until the second week in March, and once the tournament was finished, it closed for yet another year. Binnion's casino featured the highest limits in the world—and with Benny's blessing one could bet even higher; a guy named Bill Bergstrom put over seven hundred thousand dollars on the pass line at the crap table, won the bet, and then fled into the night (a great story, though rumor has it that Bergstrom was a Binnion-contrived setup and had to give the money back in secret)—and the Horseshoe was well aware that its primary profit lay in craps, blackjack, and the other player-against-the-house propositions, and setting aside the square footage required for a full-time poker room would have cut big-time into the profits from the gaming tables.

So aside from the Horseshoe itself, the main beneficiary from the old-time World Series of Poker was the Golden Nugget card room across the street, because that's where the big-timers went in between tournament events to play in the lucrative side games. Downtown Las Vegas was up to here with high players during February and March; bookmakers from around the country, their pockets stuffed with NFL Playoff and Super Bowl winnings from the previous couple of months, descended on the city in hordes, and even though the game of Hold 'Em was largely unknown to the masses in those days, most bookies played in illegal poker rooms back in their hometowns and were crazy about the game. Heavy action always attracts even more heavy action, so along with the bookies came the drug dealers (people who sell dope usually do so to feed their own addictions, one of which is high-stakes gambling) flashing even bigger bankrolls than the book-makers, with the golf hustlers, confidence men, and every known form of grafter—plus a few with scams you've never heard of—hot on their heels, ready to pick the dope guys' pockets for what-ever they could. For those of us who knew their way around the poker table, there was plenty of money to be made, though one had to proceed with caution because the wads of cash flowing through Las Vegas during the six-week period of the WSOP at-tracted the cheats as well.

If a good player could be satisfied with modestly increased profits and stick to the casino card rooms, cheating wasn't a factor in choosing where to play, but for those who craved the really big dollars, the biggest side action went on outside the casinos. Loads of money changed hands in private motel-room poker games, with even more money tossed around out at Las Vegas Coun-try Club on the golf course. I never needed a calendar to know when World Series of Poker time drew near, because when I began to see the old golf cheats I'd known at Tenison Park back in Dallas lurking around the Horseshoe and the Golden Nugget, I knew that the WSOP was just around the corner and that the poker-playing golf nuts were in for it. The Tenison guys had cheating at golf down to a science and seldom if ever got caught at it; there was one clumsy cheat, however, who very nearly got killed for his trouble, and who for the balance of his life owed his existence to the Drug Enforcement Administration (DEA).

You ready for this little tale? I'm once again straying a bit from the poker lessons, but the overall atmosphere in Las Vegas at WSOP time is something you need to appreciate.

So let me introduce Jamiel (Jimmy) Chagra, a slim, well-mannered, heavily mustachioed gentleman who blew into Las Vegas quite often from his hometown of El Paso, Texas, lugging suitcases and paper grocery sacks loaded down with hundred-dollar bills. Jimmy was from a respected El Paso family—his brothers were both lawyers—so I'm not sure exactly how he wandered off into the drug trade, but when I first met him he was the largest-scale marijuana smuggler in U.S. history and made no secret of it. A few years earlier he'd flown down to Colombia with a novel proposition: heretofore border smugglers had managed to sneak a few ounces of grass over the border tucked into their underwear, and some enterprising traffickers could get five hundred or so pounds of the stuff in through Texas's Big Bend National Park hidden on the passenger side of small, low-flying airplanes, but Jimmy wanted to bring Colombian grass into Florida three hundred thousand pounds at a time, packed down in hay underneath a freighter's hull. Jimmy did such a good sales job on his South American neighbors that the Colombian cartel fronted the expenses for the entire operation. Once the grass found its way from a pier in the Miami shipyard to various parts of the country, Jimmy and his South American contacts divided over four million dollars between them, and that was only the beginning. During the time I knew Jimmy, his eldest brother, Lee, got murdered in his downtown El Paso office, and as of today the case remains unsolved. His brother Joe—who represented Jimmy on federal conspiracy charges, at the same time as he was representing Charles Harrelson on charges that Jimmy had hired Charles to murder a federal judge in San Antonio—became the first lawyer ever bugged in the attorney visiting booth while visiting a client in jail, and he finally had to enter a guilty plea and accept a ten-year federal sentence of his own, not to mention that he had to become a prosecution stool pigeon in Harrelson's murder trial, and had to change his name and move when he got out of jail under witness protection. Joe died in a car wreck in 1996, possibly as a result of driving while looking back over his shoulder.

Jimmy traveled with an entourage of bodyguards whose main assignment was to fend off the federal drug agents who were continually on Jimmy's tail, and while the Las Vegas gamblers were terrified of the heavily armed bodyguards and the DEA, Jimmy had enough money to lose at the tables that his reputation didn't stop the gamblers from regularly fleecing the guy. He played no-limit Hold 'Em in the Horseshoe and generally brought a million dollars in cash to the table inside a briefcase, and he had one of his bodyguards stand behind him while he played in order to keep anyone from sneaking up on him from behind. And although he knew absolutely zero about the game, Jimmy's recklessness scared even the big-name players to death simply because of the size of his bankroll; it was nothing for Jimmy to straddle the blinds for twenty thousand dollars or even more (a "straddle" is a blind bet exclusive of the two forced wagers and gives the straddling player the option of raising his or her own bet after looking at his or her hand). The hustlers tried to talk Jimmy into playing something like fifteen-thousand- and thirty-thousand-dollar limit poker in order to restrict the sums he could shove into the pot all at once, but Jimmy was having none of it; he understood very well what he was up against and knew that his only legitimate chance to win was to money-whip the game. So although in the long run Jimmy donated several million dollars to the big-time poker hustlers' cause, there were individual nights when he'd draw good cards and send the world's top Hold 'Em players running for cover.

Jimmy didn't start out as a compulsive gambler, though he almost surely became one later on. During the 1970s, he had access to virtually unlimited sums of money, and at first he used the action in Las Vegas to take his mind off of other problems, which for Jimmy Chagra were countless. He was under federal indictment back in Texas for his smuggling activities, and it was while he was in Nevada that he plotted to murder the judge who was to preside over his trial. The hit man he is purported to have hired was none other than Charles Harrelson, the killer I'd known from the Amvets Club back in Dallas, and Jimmy's wife, Liz, later told federal agents that she'd delivered $250,000 to Harrelson in a Las Vegas motel room as a down payment. Someone did indeed shoot the judge to death as he left home for work on the morning that Jimmy's trial was to begin, and Harrelson was eventually convicted of the crime and sent to federal prison for life. Jimmy also suffered a federal conviction but this was for drug trafficking, not the murder; with Oscar Goodman, the future mayor of Las Vegas, acting as his lawyer, Jimmy won an acquittal on those charges. In between his conviction and sentencing, Jimmy disappeared and remained a fugitive for an entire year. During that time, with his wife as a companion, he drove a motor home through the Pacific Northwest and on into Canada, and if it hadn't been for his gambling addiction he might still be at large. He drove into Las Vegas one evening and called a pit boss he knew at the Hilton to ask that a private game be set up. Less than twenty minutes after he hung up the phone, federal agents burst into Jimmy's motel room and slapped the cuffs on him, and he was never to see life outside prison again for more than twenty years.

Actually, Jimmy's sentence was *thirty* years, but he gained an early release, because he, like his brother Joe before him, became a stool pigeon, and today he resides at points unknown under federal witness protection. He did give one interview to a reporter on the day of his release, wherein he said that Harrelson was not really the hit man. More than twenty-five years after the fact, Jimmy claimed that he and his brother Joe had falsely fingered Charles Harrelson as the judge's killer, because Charles was threatening to tell the feds that he'd done the murder under Jimmy's direction, and to testify against Jimmy unless Jimmy paid him to keep his mouth shut. You can, of course, believe Jimmy's version if you want. Personally I don't, partly because I think the idea that Joe Chagra would be a party to framing Harrelson when the deed cost Joe his law license not to mention ten years in prison is ludicrous, and partly because it's impossible to separate fact from fiction in what Jimmy Chagra has to say and always has been, but mostly because of a different tale I've heard that makes a great deal more sense to me. According to more than one source, after Harrelson had killed the judge, Jimmy reneged on his promise to come across with another quarter of a million dollars. With Harrelson putting the heat on him for the money, Jimmy was scared to death that his own name might be on Harrelson's hit list, so he tipped off Houston, Texas, cops—Harrelson was wanted in Houston on gun possession charges—as to Harrelson's whereabouts, which led to Harrelson's arrest.

But all of the murders and criminal convictions and prison sentences and whatnot came later. We're talking about things that happened while Jimmy Chagra was one of Las Vegas's most visible gamblers, and while his drug conviction was still a couple of years in the future.

While Jimmy did have an occasional run of luck at the poker table, and sometimes even at the blackjack table, the golf course was one place where Jimmy couldn't win, no way, no how. His swing could best be described as resembling the short, vicious thrusts of a man trying to kill a snake in his yard, and he might've been better off if he could've applied his putting stroke to his driver and hit off the tee with his putter, because while he seldom drove the ball past the ladies' tees, he did sometimes manage to putt the ball completely off the green. Yet he loved the game. Couldn't get enough of it. Got so hooked on golf that he began to show up every morning at Las Vegas Country Club, his henchmen strung out behind him, one of them huffing and puffing as he lugged Jimmy's clubs, ready to play as many holes as daylight would permit for as much money as anyone wanted to play for.

When a gambler with a reputation like Jimmy Chagra's takes up the game of golf, every hustler on the planet eventually finds out about it and tries to muscle in on the action, and in a place like Las Vegas the word travels like a prairie fire. One year in early February, just about time for the WSOP to kick off, a group of pirates headed out for the country club intent on taking Jimmy for every dime they could. Jimmy's main opponent that day— he generally played six in a group and had bets going with every player plus whoever wanted to tag along and take some side action—was an old Las Vegas poker legend named Puggy Pearson, who'd won the WSOP Main Event in a showdown with Johnny Moss in 1973. Puggy was a self-taught scratch golfer who could chip and putt as well as any touring pro. He agreed on the first tee, after much hemming and hawing, to give Jimmy a stroke on every hole—Jimmy probably would have needed *four* strokes a hole in order to make a match of it—for a thousand dollars per, and then Jimmy promptly accepted bets from the other four golfers in the group plus side wagers from ten or twelve spectators, so that he would have twelve to fifteen thousand dollars riding on the outcome of every single hole. And away they went,

Jimmy and Puggy in the lead, driving carts, with the other players and the spectators bringing up the rear in their own carts, looking for all the world like a gang of prairie schooners headed west.

For eight holes Jimmy's ball found nearly every water hazard, and even when his ball didn't go in a hazard, it would take him five or six strokes to get on the green, and Puggy won every hole by a comfortable margin. The match came to the ninth with Jimmy somewhere in excess of a hundred thousand dollars looser. The ninth was a medium length par 4, trees on the left and water on the right. As Puggy teed up his ball and sighted down the fairway, Jimmy said, "I want to press. You gimme a press here?"

Puggy stepped back, and you could practically see the wheels turning inside his head. He looked at Jimmy. "Press for how much?"

"Make it easy on yourself," Jimmy said.

Puggy looked down, thinking, and then slowly raised his head. "Ain't gonna letcha press to win no money. You can press to break even if you want."

"It's a bet," Jimmy said, then looked around at the other golfers and railbirds and said, "I'm pressin' all of the side bets, too."

With four of Jimmy's heavily strapped bodyguards standing menacingly nearby, no one was going to turn down any proposition that Jimmy made. The man from El Paso who couldn't break a hundred on the golf course was about to play one hole against a scratch player for more than a hundred thousand dollars. Jimmy was getting a stroke, of course, but the closest he'd come to Puggy's score on any of the previous eight holes was two.

They say that every gambling golfer has a choking point, and Jimmy apparently had just found Puggy's. The chipping and putting wizard stepped up and hit his first really bad shot of the day, a low, screaming hook that landed on the far left side of the fairway and bounded off into the woods.

Jimmy then hit his only decent drive of the day, a shot that actually got airborne for a bit, and then rolled to a stop in the center of the fairway about two hundred yards off the tee. Jimmy's entourage attaboyed and whooped it up; considering where Puggy's tee shot had gone, if their man could just make *bogey*, barring a miracle on Puggy's part, Jimmy was going to win the hole.

All the players and spectators steered their carts down the fairway. Jimmy stopped and got out when he reached his ball and began to sight toward the green, all the while standing near his bag and fingering several different clubs. Puggy rolled on ahead and off into the forest, presumably to hunt for his ball.

Jimmy figured and thought. He tossed blades of grass up into the air to check the strength and direction of the wind. Finally, he removed the head cover from a fairway wood, took his stance, and addressed the ball.

Heard faintly from over in the trees, a voice with a thick Hispanic accent said, "Stop right there, motherfucker. Don't you move."

Jimmy stepped away from his ball, his puzzled gaze off in the direction from which the voice had come. He replaced the head cover on the fairway wood, put the club away in his bag, then got in his cart and headed for the woods. The other golfers and the spectators followed right along.

The scene that greeted the cart drivers as they entered the forest: Puggy Pearson bent from the waist near a thick tree trunk frozen in his tracks with his gaze darting back and forth between the golf ball he held in his hand and Jimmy Chagra's bodyguard standing maybe ten feet away. The bodyguard had drawn his weapon, a big, mean-looking .45 clip-loaded automatic, and held it pointed at Puggy's head.

The bodyguard said, "That ball was against that tree, and this motherfucker was movin' it."

Puggy still didn't move a muscle. Jimmy tilted his head in thought.

"I'm gonna shoot the fucker if you want me to," the bodyguard said.

Jimmy looked as if he thought shooting Puggy wasn't a bad idea.

Only Puggy's lips moved as he spoke up, "I was just declarin' it unplayable."

"And that's why you picked up your ball when you thought nobody was watchin' you?" Jimmy said. "You can get killed for lyin', especially lyin' about cheatin'."

"Look," Puggy said. "Please."

At that moment a pin dropped among the leaves would have sounded like an avalanche.

Jimmy shaded his eyes and peered off into the distance. On an adjacent fairway sat two golf carts with two men in each. Jimmy said, "Don't shoot him. Could be DEA over there." (Jimmy wasn't being paranoid; just a few days after the Puggy Pearson cheating incident, a helicopter swooped down and landed in a fairway just a few yards from Jimmy's group as it played, and a federal agent got out and served Jimmy with a search warrant on his home and on his car.)

The bodyguard holstered his weapon at the small of his back. Puggy stood upright and sheepishly dropped the ball on the ground.

Jimmy took two steps toward his cart, then stopped and turned. "You forfeit the hole, motherfucker," Jimmy said. "You get caught cheatin', you gotta forfeit the hole."

And thus came to pass the only time in anyone's memory when Jimmy Chagra broke even on the golf course. His entourage packed it in, then and there, motored off to the clubhouse, and returned downtown to the Horseshoe. That night—possibly as a result of not losing on the golf course and thus being flush with more cash than usual—Jimmy booked his biggest loser ever at the poker table, more than two million dollars. Sometime in the wee hours he quit the game, stopped off at the blackjack table, played one hand for one hundred thousand dollars and won it, then collected his money and went off to bed.

And as for Puggy Pearson, he understood very well how close he came to getting killed that day, and as far as I know he never again tried to cheat on the golf course (at least not while playing against Jimmy Chagra or anyone like him). Up until then Puggy had been a regular in the poker games in which Jimmy played, but thereafter if Puggy saw the man from El Paso coming, he quickly moved to another table.

And if this golf course incident would be unheard of in the circles that you frequent, rest assured that such happenings are SOP in the professional gambler's world. I'm no angel, but the longer I was part of Las Vegas's poker society, the cheaper I felt, and as time marched on I decided that if my current circumstance was all there was to life, there wasn't enough money in the world to make it worthwhile. I didn't like having my name linked to some of the people I regularly played poker with, and I hated the way decent folk looked at me. I wanted out, even if it meant (gasp and horrors) *going back to Dallas and getting a fucking job!!!*

My ten Las Vegas years passed before I realized it; there was a sameness to every day—get up, eat midafternoon dinner, play poker all night, go to bed—that made the weeks grow into months and the months grow into years, and it seemed that I'd only blinked when an entire decade had come and gone. My short-term memory was a hodgepodge of two-card hands, beats, and drawouts, and as for any long-term recollections it seemed that I didn't have any. I think it was in about my eighth year as a Golden Nugget regular that I began to feel as if I was in a rut, but then it was two more years before a series of events, ones that came to pass over a very short period of time, completely changed my life's direction and, once and for all, put my future forays into the poker world completely under the radar.

9

Back in Civilization

or,
Las Vegas Finally Sends Me Packing

I did exactly as I was told and locked the bulging gunnysacks up in the trunk of my Cadillac. As I started to climb the stairs back up to the apartment, a horn tooted behind me. I turned, and as the black and white police car approached, my heart dropped to somewhere in the vicinity of my gonads.

I'd seen the cop who was driving the car; the apartment house paid extra for off-duty policemen to patrol, and up to now I'd felt safer with them around. I had a picture of Monkey One and Monkey Two watching a verbal exchange between me and the officer, and then going back to the bedroom and firing away. The cop waved at me. I nodded to him, then went up the steps two at a time. I left the front door open as I went inside.

Monkey One waited just inside, cradling the shotgun in the crook of his arm. He said, "You and that John Law didn't pass no signal, didja?"

I averted my gaze from him, the grinning chimpanzee snout still visible out of the corner of my eye. "He's off-duty security," I said. "He waved. I nodded."

"You sure that's all?" Monkey One said.

"Absolutely."

He held out a hand, palm up. I gave him my car keys. He gestured with the shotgun. "Lie facedown on the floor," he said.

I was shaking with fear. "Look, you don't want to do this," I said.

"Get on the floor," he said. Monkey Two came in and stood beside him. "I'm gonna count to three," Monkey One said.

I went down on my knees, then stretched out on my belly. I shut my eyes and prayed that if the guy blew my head off I'd feel no pain. Probably no more than thirty seconds passed, but it seemed to me like an eternity. I said, "What do you want me to do now?"

No one answered. I slowly opened my eyes and, sensing no presence behind me, rolled over on my back. The door was ajar, just as I'd left it. From far away, a starter chugged and an engine caught and raced. I stood and walked to the window just in time to watch my Caddy cruise slowly out of the parking lot. I didn't care about the car. I was giddy with delight just to be alive.

By the time opportunity came knocking, I'd already made up my mind to give up playing in Las Vegas as soon as I could find an alternative. During one of my two-week visits at home, I'd met the woman whom I was destined to marry—and whom I'm just as crazy in love with today as I was thirty years ago—and I could already see that trying to maintain a relationship with her while spending over half my time in Nevada wasn't going to cut it. I'd met tons of poker players in my travels who loudly claimed that "my old lady don't say nothin' about what I do or when I do it," but I'd also noticed that the guys doing that sort of bragging generally were on Old Lady Number Three or Four. I had the goofy notion that marriage would be a commitment on my part as much as it would be on hers, and that if we were to have children I should have more to do with their upbringing than merely being in the room as they were conceived. I tried taking my ladylove to Nevada along with me a couple of times, and although she did her best to be a trouper about it, I could see with one eye that she despised the place. She was and is such a tightwad—and I have only her frugality to thank for whatever it is that we have today—that the idea of losing a nickel gambling made her physically ill. She didn't drink. I took her to see Buddy Hackett at the Hilton, where she walked out in the middle of the show, because Hackett's smutty jokes disgusted her, and I also went with her to Frank Sinatra's gig at the Sands, where in the middle of Ole Blue Eyes's act she went to sleep. Her idea of a good time was completely different from what I was used to; she loved evening walks, inexpensive dinners, and idea-swapping conversation, and though my life as a high-stakes poker player had included none of the three for years and years, I was soon so much in love that her company alone was all that I ever needed. We held hands in the movies a lot. Still do. We think movies were meant to be seen in theaters, and you can keep your DVDs and good riddance. She never put any pressure on me to stop running off to Nevada to play poker, but without ever actually saying as much, she convinced me that until I was ready to commit she had plenty of other fish to fry. One weekend I flew to Dallas unannounced and decided to bowl her over by taking her to dinner. When I called her, she told me sweetly that she was so sorry but she'd made other plans. At first I thought she was joking, but she stuck firmly to her guns, and that night I found myself wandering around near her place like the guy in the old fifties song "Silhouettes on the Shade."

Even when I was in Las Vegas trying to play poker I was one lovesick puppy. I'd never played in my life when my head wasn't completely in the game, but now I just couldn't concentrate, and more than once I stared off into space for so long that a house dealer had to remind me to act on my hand.

And then out of the blue, an answer appeared. It wasn't *the* answer, and it turned out to be a pretty lousy answer, but it did get me out of Nevada and back into the real world.

One fine evening during World Series month in the Year of Our Lord 1982, I was at the Golden Nugget hooked up in a forty- and eighty-dollar limit game—twice the stakes offered year-round in the Card Room Best Known for Being Across the Street from the Horseshoe, but what the hell, it was that time of year and the high players were in town. There's a little-known fact about Las Vegas poker rooms that the public at large doesn't really appreciate: state gambling laws restrict the amount of the poker rake, and the rake doesn't go up as the betting limit increases. Since three bucks a hand is all that the game runner could knock down in those days (I believe that today the maximum allowable house rake is *four* dollars a hand), the Host Joint would have liked it better if, oh, say, three- and six-dollar limit had been as high as the action ever got. The bigger the game, the bigger the headache for the card room; not only do tempers flare and resentments smolder in direct proportion to the money at stake, but where the players' pictures are in the Poker Hall of Fame over at the Horseshoe, the large gathering of railbirds creates an additional security problem. (And here is a good place to state the reason that every casino card room in the country has gone tournament crazy today, and the reason has nothing to do with proving who's the best or any of that crapola: while in the cash games the house income is limited to its rake from the game, in a tournament, not only can the card room charge each contestant a fee over and above the buy-in, but it can also distribute the prize money so as to create a handsome profit for itself. The next time you watch a World Series event on television, compute the total purse by multiplying the number of entrants by the buy-in, and then figure the prize money by adding the various payoffs depending on where the player finishes, and you will find that the World Series game runners' profits are in the millions.) Today poker spectators sit in a cordoned-off gallery a respectful distance from the game. But back in the day, the railbirds could crowd around the table and even jockey for a peek at the players' pocket cards, so several casino heavies stood among the mob and kept an eye out for any signals passing from people in the gallery to the guys in the game.

So much does that night stand out in my mind that I can even remember some of the players at the table—Johnny Chan was one, Bobby Hoff and David Chiu were a couple of the others—and the pocket cards—AQ of hearts to go with three hearts on the board, the last of which had hit on Fifth Street to pull my chestnuts out of the fire—that had just won me the largest pot of the day, and the surge of adrenaline I felt as I arranged my chips in five-hundred-dollar stacks and let my gaze wander through the gallery for a glimpse at the reaction from my adoring fans. And there, leaning against the railing separating the poker room from the rest of the casino, stood none other than my old buddy Steve, the guy who'd found Jesus and left me holding the bag for his share of the rent during my college days.

Actually, I didn't recognize Steve at first; it had been fifteen years since I'd seen him and he just didn't look like the same guy I'd known. As a football jock he'd been deep chested and broad shouldered, but now he was skinny as a drinking straw and sported a beard. My initial reaction was, hey, who is the guy who keeps on staring at me and where have I seen him before? Then Steve raised a hand and waggled his fingers in my direction, a mannerism of his that hadn't changed, and all at once I knew who he was.

I looked quickly away. Remember that this was the guy who'd spouted off about religion like a lunatic and stiffed me for half the rent on a pretty expensive apartment. *Christ*, I thought, *is the guy going to start preaching a sermon?* I pretended not to notice him.

My ploy didn't work, of course. Steve circled the table until he stood behind me, poked my arm. I made up my mind that if he started to speak in Holy Roller tongues, or if his head started spinning around like the kid in *The Exorcist,* I was making a run for it.

Steve bent close and whispered, "You got a minute?"

I calmed down some. He didn't sound crazy, and if I could steer him away from the poker table and to the privacy of the bar it wouldn't matter if he did turn out to be a nut; I knew the bouncers and how to signal them. I thought he was probably about to touch me for some money, and if he didn't ask for too much it might be a cheap way to get rid of the guy. I stood and led the way to the casino bar just inside the Golden Nugget entry with Steve on my heels. We sat side by side. He ordered a Scotch and I ordered a Coke. I said to him, "Now look, I'm no more religious than the last time you saw me."

And Steve said, offhandedly, "I'm not into that shit. Not anymore."

Christ, the guy had come full circle. Now I waited for him to hit me up.

"I'm back playing poker again," Steve said.

He'd just exceeded my loan limit, and he hadn't yet asked for a loan. Fifty or a hundred bucks, yeah, but the buy-in to the game in which I was playing was a thousand dollars, minimum, and no way would I advance him that much. I said, "Look, Steve, I gotta be—"

I stopped in midsentence as the bartender delivered our drinks. Steve said, "Let me get this." He pulled a wad of money out of his pocket that would choke an elephant. The bills I could see were mostly hundreds. He thumbed through the money, located a ten, gave it to the bartender, and told her to keep the change.

So Steve was flush with cash. Ole Steve, who woulda thought it? More importantly, what did he want with me? Many years had passed, but I still had no reason to trust this guy.

He said, "I got a proposition for you."

I thumbed toward the poker room. "I'm on my own in poker, if you—"

"I don't want part of your action, either," Steve said. "I can finance my own action. I want you to go in with me running a poker game."

Now I shot a long, meaningful glance in the direction of the poker room, then swiveled my head to look at the street outside. Visible through the open entryway, World Series contestants lounged around near the street exit from the Horseshoe. "In case you haven't noticed," I said, "there's a little competition around here."

"I'm not talking about here," Steve said. "I'm talking about Dallas."

I blinked. Now Steve had my attention. I said, "I gotta tell you, I started playing in Nevada about ten years ago because it was safer, no hijacks, cheats, and whatnot. If I have anything to do with a Texas operation, there's gotta be security."

Steve waved a hand as if batting at mosquitoes. "Your problem is, you spent too much time around joints like the Amvets. Those guys, those players, they're barred from the game I'm talking about. We deal strictly with business types. Guys we knew from college, and people they'll vouch for."

"Those old jockstraps," I said. I was picturing guys drawing light without the money to cover their losses, and the house having to match their chips to satisfy the other players.

"Things since college have changed, and some of those guys are substantial. Plus there are all those old Phi Delts."

"Oh, for a room full of those Phi Delt guys," I said.

"So you're interested?" he said.

"I might be." I frowned. "How did you know where to find me?"

"I stopped by the Amvets one day. Some of those guys had seen you in Vegas and told me if I came to the Nugget I stood a good chance of running into you."

"*Las* Vegas," I said. "The natives out here insist on using the whole name of the town. Look, on the one hand, you're saying that this game you're talking about bars any pros, then, on the other hand, you're talking about contact with the Amvets. If those pros know this game is going on, how you gonna keep them away?"

"They don't know there's a game," Steve said. "They just know I asked about you."

I scratched my head. "Christmas has come and gone. So why are you so generous all of a sudden? I'll tell you up front, I'm not interested in something like we did way back when, with you doing nothing and getting ninety percent."

Steve spread his hands like in an umpire's "safe" signal. "Strictly fifty-fifty. This thing is getting too big for one man. Every night, I'm losing so much sleep I'm a zombie. I had to shut the thing down for a few days just to come out here and find you. You're a guy I trust. Not too many people you can trust in this business."

He could say that again. The problem was, I counted Steve among the group that I couldn't trust. I said, "I get first count on the money."

"Suit yourself," he said.

I looked at the ceiling, then down at my folded hands. "Tell you what. I'm planning to fly to Dallas in a couple of days. You got a phone number?"

He reached in his pocket and handed me a slip of paper. "Already wrote it down for you. Look, it would mean you sticking around town and not be flying off to Nevada all the time."

"Flying to Las Vegas is what I'm trying to get away from," I said. "Give you an answer in four days. Listen, I gotta get back to the game before I lose my seat."

"Don't let me hold you up," Steve said. "Call me, huh?" He left the bar and started heading for the casino exit.

"Hey," I said.

He stopped and turned back toward me.

"What happened to Jesus?" I asked.

He seemed in thought. Finally, he smiled. "Faith don't feed nobody," he said. "Money does." He started to walk away again. "Don't forget to call me," he said over his shoulder.

I folded the slip of paper containing his number, tucked it away, and headed back for the poker room. I still had my doubts as to whether Steve was on the level, but, I had to admit, he talked a pretty good game.

10

Life Among the Amateurs

The uniformed cop looked over the poker table, the chips and cards scattered about, and said, "We oughtta bust your ass for runnin' a poker game."

Which was typical of police cooperation after poker game robberies. In those days, most game runners didn't call the cops after they'd been hijacked, for the very reason that police acted as if they thought the incident was funny, and normally wouldn't even go through the motions of investigating. I'd debated long and hard with myself before calling 911 and wouldn't have if it hadn't been for the insistence of one of the players. This guy was a square-john type who had lost a couple of pretty valuable pieces of jewelry during the robbery, and who, unlike 99 percent of the poker players I knew, actually had insurance. His insurance company required that the cops be called before it would pay off his claim. I'd even thought about reimbursing the guy out of my pocket, but that would have brought up any number of problems, such as the other players would have thought if I was paying the other guy, why leave them out. Also, I'd learned that the guy had insured the jewelry for twenty thousand dollars, and that figure had spurred me to go ahead and call in the law. But now I almost wished I hadn't.

I decided to tell a big fat lie, and I stood up from the chair in which I sat. I said to the cop, "Now, we're not running any poker game up here. We don't cut the pot or anything; this is just a bunch of friends renting an apartment so we could play every week and stay out of our wives' hair."

The officer exchanged a look with his partner. Clearly they didn't believe me.

I said, "Why, you got proof to the contrary? Hey, if you don't want to write a report . . ."

Obviously they had no proof that I was doing anything illegal. If they had, I would've already been headed downtown in a squad car. The officer at first looked irritated, then totally disgusted, but finally produced a spiral notebook. "I'll write up a report," he said. "What the robbery detectives want to do with the report, that's up to them."

A week later I was back on my home turf running a poker game with my old college cohort Steve as a partner, and it dawned on me that I hadn't made much progress in the past twenty years. The money was better, of course, and in the times I was able to play in the game I could see that the profits from playing could be more than the rake. But other than looking and feeling older, I had the same life as I had had when Steve and I had shared an apartment back in college: set up the poker table and drinks and snacks daily by one P.M., run sandwiches and drinks to the players while Steve acts as house dealer, spell Steve every few hours so that he can sleep, stay up all night and sleep in late, and then begin the same routine all over again. Christ, the faces were even the same: two of my old buddies from the athletic dorm, Raw Meat and the sore-assed running back, were among the players, not to mention most of the regulars who'd played in the Phi Delt game. And though nearly all of our old college compadres had become businessmen or lawyers—one guy was even a surgeon—they hadn't improved one iota as poker players. My first three days back in Dallas I won a thousand dollars in addition to my share of the rake.

There were major problems over the rake. Steve might've shed his Jesus robes, but he was just as full of bullshit as he'd ever been; in spite of the promises he'd made sitting at the bar in the Golden Nugget, when it came time to split the money it was like pulling teeth to get my fair share. I've met others in my life who aren't happy unless they're trying to get over on someone, but Steve was the worst I've ever seen. If the total rake was, say, a thousand dollars, he'd try giving me four hundred and keeping the rest for himself, and if I questioned the split he'd moan about his setup expenses and claim that as dealer he was entitled to the lion's share because dealing was more important than waiting on the players. My approach to solving the problem was to pocket the entire rake I took while I was dealing and make Steve come to me for his share, rather than the other way around. And whatever he'd shorted me when divvying the portion of the rake during his turn at dealing, I'd short him the same amount when divvying the rake from mine, which made us equal participants in the profits but didn't make for really pleasant harmony. A week had yet to pass before I'd started casting around for something else to do.

My main reason for wanting to abandon Las Vegas was to improve my love life, but now things were worse between my future wife and me than they'd ever been. When I'd been spending the lion's share of my time in Nevada, she'd known that we couldn't be together except every couple of weeks or so, but now that Dallas was my base once again, she'd rightfully assumed that I'd have more time for her. But, in fact, the opposite was true; except for ducking out to take her to dinner every couple of days, and crashing at her place when I wasn't helping Steve with the game—which took up, at a minimum, sixteen hours a day of my time—I never saw her.

If you're getting the idea that life as a poker player/game runner is tough on relationships, then you have about half of this chapter's lesson down pat and have earned an A on that part. I was unhappy in love and I was so disgusted with Steve that other than arguing with him over the money split, I'd just about quit speaking to the guy.

Money doesn't buy happiness, folks. I'd stuffed my pockets with so much cash that I listed when I walked, yet I was more miserable than I'd ever been. The arrangement with Steve wasn't working out on any number of levels, but I'd yet to see the worst of it. The straw that broke the camel's back came out of the blue.

It happened around one in the morning after I'd been in- volved in running the game for just about three weeks. That very afternoon, in fact, I'd talked to a man about renting space in his then-unoccupied farmhouse and starting a game of my own. I hadn't finalized the new deal as yet and wasn't planning to tell Steve about the proposed change until I had, but some- thing was about to happen to alter my plans.

I'd just taken over the dealing duties from Steve. I'd scooped the deck together and begun to shuffle, all the while glancing around to make a ballpark estimate of the chips out to the play- ers and the amount in chips in the rack in front of me. Truth be told, I'm a pretty good Hold 'Em dealer, though in my cur- rent vagabond pigeon status I never let that fact be known. I get along well with the players and have been known to knock down plenty of tips—though not in a game with my old college buddies, who, in full-blown bluenose university graduate mode, would think that by tipping me they'd be insulting me. And you know what? They were right. I would have been insulted, though not for the reason that they would be thinking. Knowing those guys, any tips they gave would be about a fourth of what I deserved.

Steve had left the room as soon as I'd spelled him, and I'd assumed he was headed for the john. As I dealt out ten two-card Hold 'Em hands, Steve returned with two new guys in tow. I looked the guys over, then concentrated like hell on the deck in my hand.

Raw Meat hit some impossible drawout and won the pot. As I shoved the pile of chips over in front of Raw Meat, Steve and the newcomers leaned against the wall. Steve and one of the guys had their arms folded and the other guy had his hands jammed into his pockets. I gathered up the cards in preparation for shuffling and pointedly ignored Steve and his buddies.

Finally, Steve called my name. I looked up, and I'm sure he could tell that I was pissed. Nonetheless, he thumbed toward the man on his left as he said, "You remember Roy," then indicated the guy on his right and said, "and D.R., don'tcha?"

I damned sure did. Roy and D.R. were perfect examples of people whom I'd hoped to never see again. In the old days, they'd been peripheral characters around the Amvets Club, non–poker players who showed up occasionally and sat around watching the action, and who gave me goose bumps and sent me home in a hurry whenever they arrived. D.R. had done Mississippi time for burglary, that much I knew, though I'd heard from several sources that his specialty wasn't breaking and entering but strong-arm robbery (beating up people and taking their money), though he'd rather stick a gun in his victim's face if he happened to be packing—though getting his hands on a firearm was sometimes tough for D.R. because of his police record. D.R.'s sidekick Roy was an old-time Benny Binnion cohort from the 1940s who had moved to Las Vegas shortly after Benny had bought the Horseshoe. Roy had operated a sports book for a number of years in

Nevada, and I'd heard that he'd returned to Dallas a few years back and was now the principal operator of the Amvets game, with D.R. as his Number Two Guy. The word on Roy was that he'd killed more people in his life than Charley Boyd and Charles Harrelson combined, though through fifty-something arrests he'd yet to have a conviction hung on him. The guys whom Steve had just brought into the room were a couple of real sweet potatoes, the very same folks whom Steve had sworn to me in Las Vegas he was keeping this poker game a secret from. Score another lie for good ole Steve.

I kept on dealing, so mad at Steve that I was afraid that if I looked his way I'd do something I'd later regret. The players were too caught up in the game to notice who'd come in and who'd left, and besides, the business types in this poker game didn't run in the same circles as Roy and D.R., so they wouldn't know them from Adam. But I knew them from Adam, and the fact that the players in the game didn't know D.R. or Roy didn't make their bankrolls one bit safer.

I went on putting out Hold 'Em hands for another hour while Steve took D.R. and Roy into the living room for a bullshit session. Finally, Steve showed up to spell me. I stuck the chips I'd raked from the game in my pocket, just as always. As I stood to surrender my seat at the table, I whispered to Steve, "We're gonna talk later on." He didn't answer, just sat down and prepared to shuffle the cards, and wouldn't meet my gaze as I backed away from the table. I turned on my heel and went down the hall.

After I'd stopped to use the bathroom, I went on to the front of the apartment to find D.R. and Roy still seated on the sofa in the living room. It would have been pointless for me to ignore these two fine citizens, so I nodded hello. Roy pointed a thick finger at a chair across a low coffee table from D.R. and him and told me to sit. It wasn't an invitation; it was an order; I sat.

D.R. was blind in one eye and wore a patch. I'd heard that he'd lost the eye in a knife fight, decades ago. He had thick red hair going to gray. He bent from the waist and rested his forearms on his thighs. "You gotta cut us in on this," he said, jerking his head toward the back of the apartment, where the poker game was going on.

Anyone who wasn't afraid of D.R. was probably just as crazy as he was. I swallowed hard and tried to ignore the butterflies in my stomach as I said, "It's not my game to cut you in on. I'm just dealing and running food and drinks. You talk to Steve?"

Roy draped one arm over the sofa back and crossed his legs. He hadn't shaved in a day or two and had a front tooth missing. He said, "Yeah, we talked. And he told us to ask you. Said it was your game. If you two don't know whose game it is, maybe we should just take over the whole thing."

Muscling in on someone else's racket wasn't exclusive to the Mafia; though underworld characters in Dallas weren't as organized as their back-east counterparts, they were just as dangerous if not more so. A New York mobster wouldn't dream of starting a protection racket without the capo's approval, and even if the head man gave his blessing, the underboss would restrict his activities to a certain territory in order to keep from stepping on some other family's toes. Dallas hoodlums pulled their strong-arm tactics whenever and wherever they pleased, and if they happened to be in some other gangster's territory, so be it; they'd settle the issue with gunfire. Back when Benny Binnion ran Dallas, he was in a continual turf war with a Fort Worth mobster named Herbert Noble; after Noble had survived so many attempts on his life that Binnion's people hung him with the nickname "The Cat" (nine lives, get it?), a bomb finally did him in one morning as he opened his mailbox.

I'd run other poker games, though never for more than a year at a time, and I'd yet to be in partnership with gangsters and wasn't about to start now. But as I said in an earlier chapter, where states refuse to legalize gambling, really dangerous people take control of the illegal casinos and poker rooms, and as long as I continued to ply my trade in Dallas, contact with gangsters was unavoidable. I didn't want to be out of business, especially since I'd only started three weeks earlier, but I would rather have turned the game over to this pair than start kicking back to them. I said, "Well, maybe I'd better talk to Steve."

"What's to talk?" D.R. said. "You can cut us in, or we can start running the game ourselves."

This last threat was a bluff; D.R. and Roy weren't dumb, and they realized full well that if a couple of hoods started running the game, the square-john players would be frightened to death and disappear in a hurry. They needed Steve, and especially me, to stick around in order for the game to keep going on. Well, they could count on their buddy Steve, but if these thugs took over the game, I'd be gone in a heartbeat. Not that I was about to say as much; people who confront folks like D.R. and Roy are making a serious mistake and often pay for their errors with broken arms or legs or even a dunk in the lake while wearing a cement bathing suit. That might be an overly dramatic way of describing the situation, but them's the facts as they are.

I told Roy and D.R. that they'd have their answer within forty-eight hours. Two days should give me enough time to finalize the deal on renting the farmhouse, and haul a couple of poker tables and chip racks out to the country in order to set up my own game. I said good-bye to the thugs, went back to the poker room, and took a few drink and food orders. When I next passed through the living room, Roy and D.R. were gone.

The game broke up around dawn and the door had barely closed on the last player to leave before I poked Steve in the chest with a stiffened finger. "You're a lying son of a bitch," I said. "You know that, don't you?"

He licked his lips and looked as if he was about to tell me still another one, then apparently changed his mind. He watched the floor. "Roy and D.R., they fronted me a little money."

I began to pace back and forth. "Jesus Christ, I should have known. You were broke and went to them for a loan, and they've been in on this game from the get-go. It was them that sent you to Las Vegas after me, because they knew that with this particular group of players they couldn't just send in some on-parole dealer to help you out. How'm I doing?"

Steve continued to look at his feet, and didn't answer.

I spun to face him. "How much do you owe them?"

"Aww . . . Hey, I don't owe 'em nothin'. Not, uh, not exactly."

I looked at the ceiling. I now had the answer to some questions that had really stumped me up to now. I looked at Steve. "D.R. and Roy fronted expense money to start the game, so they've had a piece of the action all along, and that's why you've been trying to short me on my end of the rake, so you could keep on giving them their end. So since I wouldn't go for getting shorted, now you've had to level with them about what you told me in Nevada to suck me in, so in order to get what part of the action they were supposed to be getting all along, they had to help you cook up a bullshit story about how they were just now muscling in. Well, nice try, but I'm not buying it. I'm not gonna be in partnership with those two, and after tonight I'm not gonna be in with you, either."

"Let me talk to them," Steve said.

"And say what? That the three of you need to dream up more bullshit to keep me on the string? I'm going, Steve. I'll stay on through tomorrow to give you a chance to dig up a substitute, but after that you won't see me anymore."

Steve looked desperate. "Maybe you could buy us all out."

"I don't wanna buy you out. I wanna get the hell away from you."

"Come on," Steve said. "You might be putting me up shit creek with those two guys."

"You're breaking my heart," I said.

"Those two assholes, they might hurt me," Steve said.

"And you know what? That's your problem, and I sort of hope they do. I'm outta here, Steve. I'll do the game tomorrow night, but after that it's *adios*, motherfucker."

"Look, can't we talk?"

"Bye, Steve," I said. I walked out the door and left him standing there. I wouldn't have wanted to be in Steve's shoes just then, but he'd made his own bed and all that crap. He could lie in the mess or run like hell, and at that moment I couldn't have cared less what happened to him.

I went over to my sweetheart's pad and crashed, but I didn't get much sleep and sure as hell didn't like being in bed alone. She had a job, dammit. In addition to the problems with Steve—not to mention Roy and D.R.—I was scared to death of losing her, and I wouldn't have blamed her if she'd tossed my belongings out in the street and gone off in search of someone who appreciated her more. I decided then and there that keeping her was my number one priority, and to hell with everything else in my life.

Actually, I hadn't agreed to stay on with Steve for one more day out of the goodness of my heart. Neither was I doing it in an attempt to be fair, to give Steve the opportunity to replace me, or any other of the fictional motives that guys use in business in order to bullshit each other while one of them is getting screwed. The method in my madness had to do with the players in the game. I was confident that if I rented the farmhouse, Steve's game would collapse with me gone, and then I could lure his players over to my own game. In this regard I wasn't really thinking straight, because once D.R. and Roy would discover where my new game was located—and they would; once they made up their minds to, there was no way in hell to keep them from it—they'd be paying me a none too friendly visit. If I'd had time to work on things, I would have kept Roy and D.R. in mind while I'd developed Plan B.

But I never had the chance to think things out, did I?

I may have dozed for an hour or so before my alarm blasted me back into reality. I had just enough time to jump in and out of the shower and head off to reopen the game, for the very last time, before the sun went down. My heart wouldn't be into all of the glad-handing of my old college friends that I was going to have to do, but I was determined to finish out my deal with Steve without alienating any potential customers. I bathed and shaved, climbed wearily into my clothes, stumbled out to my car, and away I went.

I reached the apartment house; parked at the bottom of the steps, as always; and jogged upstairs to our poker-playing pad. Normally, I'm pretty vigilant when going to or from an illegal poker game, but today I had my mind on Steve and how happy I'd be to get away from him. I unlocked the door, walked straight back to the bedroom where the poker table stood, stopped, and looked around. As always, cards were scattered across the table and strewn around on the floor. There were trash bags in the closet along with a vacuum cleaner, and I took one step in that direction. As I did, Monkey One stepped out from his hiding place and pointed a sawed-off over-and-under shotgun at me. "On the floor," he said.

11

I Lose My Car for Good and Finally Find Refuge as a Member of the Permanent Pigeons' Club

That's about it as far as my life as a know-all-of-the-dealers-and-housemen-and-con-men-and-hit-men-on-a-first-name-basis, pal-around-with-the-stars, big-shot professional poker player, and I've got to say that with twenty-plus years away from that life to look back on, I don't miss those days one iota. Within a five-mile radius of the house we live in today are four illegal backroom poker parlors that I know of, plus, I'm sure, others that I'm unaware of since I don't go in search of such places any longer. Many people whom I once counted among my closest friends still play in those joints, but every time I'm tempted to reacquaint myself, I picture my home, my wife, and my children and think better of it. Life as a poker star simply requires too much all-night time in smoke-filled rooms and too much sack time during the day to build any sort of family unit; the full-time professional poker players I've known over the years who've gotten married and stayed that way are rare, rare birds. I don't play poker nearly as much as I used to and spend nearly every night at home, but I've learned to make the most of the times that I am in action, so that although my income isn't near what it once was as a player, I still have plenty of money to get by on.

Re the hijacking that scared me straight: Since my old buddy Steve never showed up for the game that day, it's a dead certainty that he was in on the robbery, though it's just as dead certain that D.R. and Roy were the ones actually giving Monkey One and Monkey Two their marching orders, since Steve sure as hell didn't have the balls and didn't know anyone who did. It takes a lot of guts to rob a poker game when you're going to have to hold a roomful of men captive for several hours, and though my hat certainly isn't off to Monkey One and Monkey Two, I can appreciate that pulling a successful hijacking requires a specialist type of guy. Since Steve was the only one other than me with a key to that apartment, and since there was no sign of forced entry on the robbers' part, the finger of guilt can point to no one other than Steve and his partners in crime. I've never laid eyes on Steve since that day, though to be truthful I haven't really been on the lookout for the guy, so it's possible that he's walked right by me in some card room or another, and I never noticed him when he did. If I did see him face-to-face, he wouldn't be in for any warm hellos from me.

My spanking-new white El Dorado never turned up and probably ended its days dismantled in some chop shop with the parts shipped to points around the world. My insurance company paid me about half what the car was worth—with the claims adjuster showing up on my doorstep with the draft (two weeks later than promised) adding insult to injury by telling me he was *glad to be of fucking service*—but getting gypped on that deal was probably best for me. I bought a used Chevrolet with the money and continue to drive inexpensive, low-key vehicles to this day. Pimps, dope peddlers, and poker players stand out like sore thumbs because of their flashy rides.

For a few weeks after the robbery, I couldn't sleep at night and imagined every creak in the ceiling or walls to be Monkey One and Monkey Two about to drop in on me again. Fortunately, I had enough money that I didn't need any income for a while, so I could take my time in considering my options. My lady and I were married a month to the day after the hijacking, and since my life up to that point had pretty much been a series of aimless wanderings, I have to place my wedding date far ahead of my birthday when it comes to my lifetime highlight reel.

I thought of a lot of things that I might do for a living over the following months, including getting a job, and I even set up a few interviews. The problem was my nonexistent work experience; in the fourteen years since my college graduation I hadn't hit a lick that I could tell an interviewer about, and other than some guys who hung around a poker joint all day and some others whose pictures turned up regularly on post office walls, I was completely out of references. The few times that I actually got around to discussing salary during an interview, the figure that those companies were talking wouldn't have been enough for me to get by on anyhow, so I console myself over my lack of offers by telling myself that I didn't want their old jobs to begin with.

My future wife made no bones about the fact that running a poker game was out of the question for me if she was to be included in my life, and though, at the time, I thought she was being a bit ridiculous, today I'm glad that I've never set up another illegal game. Things have changed drastically for the back-street game runners in recent years, largely because of the influence of the folks who have the legal games. My home state, Texas, is now surrounded on three sides (the fourth side borders Mexico, both the Republic of and the Gulf of) by states where poker is legal. Legal poker parlors are associated with casinos whose owners have very deep pockets, and those owners don't hesitate to spread the wealth among political hopefuls in neighboring states in the form of campaign donations, the result being the kind of law enforcement crackdowns on the backstreet games that never existed in the old days. If the legal casinos can eliminate competition from illegal sources, then Texans who want to play poker will have to drive across the border to do so. It used to be that raids only happened in election years, but now Dallas cops are busting poker parlors right and left, and whereas the punishments used to be mere fines and probation, today some of the game runners are actually going to jail.

Since running a poker game was out, and since my job outlook was pretty bleak, I began to cast about for something else to do. I knew I could make a living playing poker (or at least I'd survived for many years doing just that), and my only problem with being a poker pro had to do with the places I'd have to frequent and the criminal element I'd be exposed to by doing so. I talked things over with my wife. She had no problem with me being a poker player, but she insisted that I do so in places where I wouldn't be arrested or killed.

A decade and a half earlier I'd played for several years at a golf club located between Dallas and Fort Worth near the Six Flags Amusement Park, and though the pickings at the club had been good, I'd eventually given in to the lure of Las Vegas and the bright lights and my chance to associate with all of the Big-Time Poker Guys. The golf club was still there, and the people playing in the poker game were essentially the same bunch as I'd known before, so one afternoon I drove out to the club and had a look around. It turned out that the club desperately needed members and was in the throes of a membership drive, so I rejoined the club for what amounted to a song and played in the poker game that very afternoon. I won a couple thousand dollars that first day, and after a really profitable couple of weeks playing in the afternoon with players who weren't likely to run in a cold deck or stick a gun in my face, and getting home before sundown every evening, I pretty well gave up the job hunt. A few times since then I've held a job, but never for very long.

Over the next few years, I expanded my horizons, and while I did avoid Las Vegas, just as I'd vowed to, I made numerous forays into California (which had finally changed its law so as to allow stud poker in its card rooms, which in short order led to some of the softest Texas Hold 'Em action on the continent) and Atlantic City, where the action was tougher than in California, largely due to the guys from the New York City underground games who flocked there on the weekends. Over the next several years, I alternated among California, Atlantic City, and Dallas, switching locations often enough so that no one ever thought of me as a regular in any particular poker game. As the years passed and one state after another began to legalize casinos, which, in turn, establish poker rooms, I found even more places where I could earn a decent living without blowing my cover. I've played in Mississippi, Louisiana, Oklahoma, New Mexico, and Arizona in recent years, and I believe this country has finally reached the point where no one who wants to play poker should have to do so illegally ever again.

So while the poker life of forty years ago has gone the way of outdoor toilets and passed into ancient history, those old-time games still make for some fascinating tales, and the proper winning strategy in poker hasn't changed one iota. As a modern-day player, be glad that you don't have to travel the same roads as many of us did, and here's hoping that you can profit from some of our bygone experiences. I know that those experiences helped me to grow, and here's hoping that you pick up enough from my writing that those experiences may do the same for you.

Made in the USA
Lexington, KY
22 February 2016